# HOME HANDYMAN
# ELECTRICS AND LIGHTING

AURA
BOOKS

# CONTENTS

Editor: Mary Lambert
Designer: Eljay Crompton

This edition published by
Aura Book Distribution Limited
2 Derby Road
Greenford, Middlesex

Produced by
Marshall Cavendish Books Limited
58 Old Compton Street
London W1V 5PA

© Marshall Cavendish Limited 1984
ISBN 0 86307 258 5
Printed and bound in Milan, Italy by New Interlitho

---

**Electricity—the law and you**

In the UK, regulations covering wiring are compiled by the Institute of Electrical Engineers. Anyone may do his own wiring, but the IEE regulations must be complied with. These require that major electrical installations should be inspected, tested and certified by a 'competent person' such as a qualified electrician or your local electricity board. Minor improvements do not need to be certified, provided they follow the IEE regulations.

**If in doubt, consult a qualified electrician**

Electrical regulations stated apply to the UK only and for 240 volt single phase supply

---

While every care has been taken to ensure that the information in Home Handyman is accurate, individual circumstances may vary greatly. So proceed with caution when following instructions, especially where electrical, plumbing or structural work is involved

*Electrics and Lighting* **takes you through all the most popular electrical jobs around the house, from installing sockets and switches to wiring up cookers and electric showers. For the security-conscious, there's a section on how to install your own burglar alarm. There is also advice on lighting indoors and outside**

# How electricity works

Electricity in the home is something which we all take for granted—and would be lost without. Yet electricity is also highly dangerous if it is not treated with the respect it deserves. For the do-it-yourself enthusiast, this means having a sound knowledge of the way in which domestic installations work before tackling any electrical job with confidence.

## Electricity and the law

In the UK, regulations covering wiring are compiled by the Institute of Electrical Engineers. Anyone may do his own wiring, but the IEE regulations must be complied with. These require that all electrical installations be tested on completion by the relevant electricity supply board.

## Electrical measures

An electric current consists of a flow of minute particles called electrons. This flow can be likened to the flow of water from a tap connected by a pipe to a tank.

For water to flow when the tap is opened, the tank must be at a higher level than the tap. And the greater the height of the tank, the higher the pressure of the water that comes out of the tap. So water at high pressure has a greater rate of flow, or current, than water at low pressure.

The *voltage* in an electrical circuit corresponds with the *pressure* of the water in the pipe. The *rate* of flow of an electric current is measured in *amperes* and is equivalent to the flow of water along the pipe—that is, how much comes out at any given time.

Electrical power is measured in *watts*. This term applies to the electrical equipment itself and is a measurement of the rate at which it uses electricity. An average electric light bulb uses only about 100 watts, whereas a powerful electric heater might use 3,000 watts

**Below:** Electricity enters the house through an armoured service cable connected to the company fuse. From here, power flows through to the meter

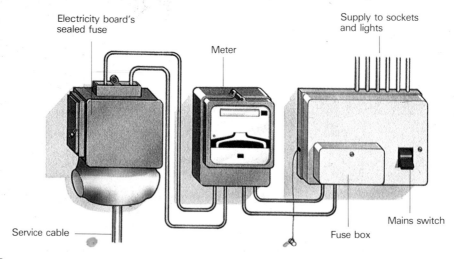

Electricity board's sealed fuse

Meter

Supply to sockets and lights

Service cable

Fuse box

Mains switch

**A:** Power runs to an electrical appliance via the live wire and actually returns via the neutral wire. To be a double safeguard against electric shocks, the switch to the appliance is always placed on the 'live' side. The earth wire carries power to earth in an emergency

**B:** For a wall switch, the live current must be diverted down the wall and back again. Usually a standard two-wire cable is used, with wires of — confusingly — different colours. But both of these wires are in fact 'live' connections. A separate earth wire is connected to the rose

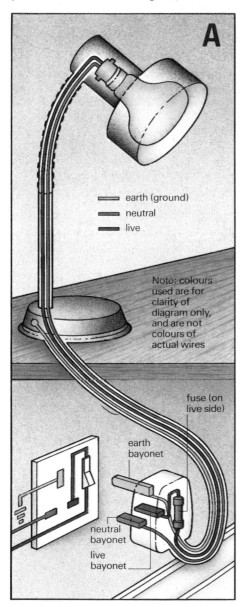

A

— earth (ground)
— neutral
— live

Note: colours used are for clarity of diagram only, and are not colours of actual wires

fuse (on live side)

earth bayonet

neutral bayonet

live bayonet

B

— earth (ground)
— neutral
— live

These wires usually combined in one outer cable

Note: colours used are for clarity of diagram only, and are not colours of actual wires

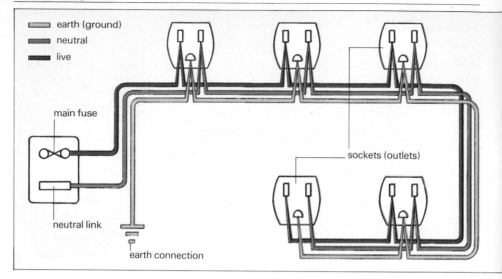

- earth (ground)
- neutral
- live

main fuse

sockets (outlets)

neutral link

earth connection

(3 kilowatts). The relationship between amps, volts and watts is expressed in the formula:

$$\frac{\text{Watts}}{\text{Volts}} = \text{Amps}$$

This formula is useful for determining both the correct size of cable to use for an appliance and, in British systems, the correct size of cartridge fuse inserted in its plug.

### Domestic installations

The comparison between the flow of water in a pipe and an electric current in a wire is not exact: electricity requires a closed loop—a circuit—in order to work.

Electricity comes into the home from a local transformer through an armoured service cable or via overhead wires. The service cable is connected to a fuse unit—called the company fuse—which is sealed by the electricity board or company. From here, power flows along the live supply wire and through the meter to the consumer unit—a combined fuse box and main switch, one particular type of which is shown on page 2. The live supply wire is usually encased in two

# Loop circuit

**C:** A typical loop electrical circuit, with each light or power outlet 'looped off' from the one before it. In circuits throughout Britain, the live wire is red, the neutral black, and the earth is bare copper covered with a green/yellow striped PVC sleeve whenever it is exposed. Loop circuits are not very common in Britain—the radial or ring main system is far more usual. Most loop circuits are, in fact, radial circuits which have been extended to create more socket outlets. The ground wire is bare copper, sometimes terminating in a green plastic-covered 'jumper'

separate sheaths. The electricity then flows through your lights and appliances before returning to the local transformer along the neutral wire. A third wire, the earth, connects the appliance casing to the main fuse box casing and then to the ground. Unless a fault develops in the system, it carries no current.

### Loop circuits

In the US and Canada—and most other

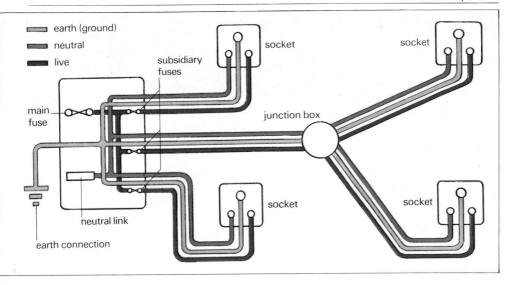

earth (ground)
neutral
live

subsidiary
fuses

socket

socket

main
fuse

junction box

neutral link

socket

socket

earth connection

# Radial circuit

**D:** A radial circuit of the type used in all British installations before 1947. The wire colours are exactly the same—red (live), black (neutral) and green/yellow (earth) as in newer wiring, but the sockets have no fuses at all, being protected instead by the fuses at the main switchboard. When re-wiring, the metal conduit from the old system is often useful as a means of feeding new wires through the wall plaster. But the ends of this metal conduit often have to be cut off so they cannot possibly touch any of the wires in either the new sockets or in the switches

parts of the world—power and lighting outlets are served by a system called *loop* wiring (fig. C). In this system the live, neutral and earth wires run outwards from the main switch to the first light (or power socket). From there they are 'looped off' to the second light; from the second light to the third; and so on. The number of lights and/or power outlets on each circuit is limited by local ordinances, so that every house needs a

number of circuits. In some such systems, an individual circuit will supply both lighting and power outlets. In others, the lighting circuits and those that supply wall sockets (for appliances and so on) are separate installations.

In the UK, lighting circuits are still of the loop type. And up until 1947, power circuits were also of a similar type called *radial* wiring, in which each socket was served by a live, neutral and earth cable direct from the main fuse board. These older British systems are fitted with three varieties of round pin sockets rated at 15 amps, 5 amps and 2 amps. The configuration of the pins is the same in all three cases but reduces in size with current rating.

In all loop and radial systems, because the plugs that fit the sockets have no fuse of their own to help protect appliances, the circuit fuses in the fuse box must be kept to as low an amp rating as possible in order to give both the cable and the appliance a reasonable degree of protection from overload.

### Ring-main system

In Britain, houses wired since 1947 use, for power socket circuits only, a different

5

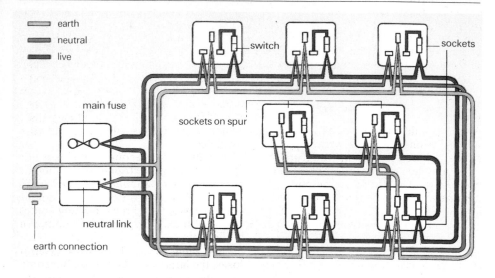

earth
neutral
live

switch

sockets

main fuse

sockets on spur

neutral link

earth connection

wiring system known as the *ring main* circuit (fig. E). In this system, the live, neutral and earth wires run in a complete circle from the main switch to each socket in turn, and then back to the consumer unit. There is generally one ring for each floor of a house, with 'spurs' reaching out from it to supply isolated sockets and appliances.

Plugs and socket outlets in ring-main circuits are of the 13 amp rectangular pin type. These are much safer than the old round-pin types because the sockets have shutters inside which automatically close when a plug is withdrawn. Furthermore, ring main plugs, unlike other types, carry their own cartridge fuses. This means that should an individual appliance become faulty, only the fuse in its own plug—and not the main fuse for the whole circuit—will 'blow' and break the circuit.

### Earthing

Should a live wire come into contact with the metal casing of an appliance, anyone who touches the appliance is liable to receive a severe electric shock. For this reason, domestic appliances—apart from ones that are double insulated

# Ring main

E: The ring main is a circuit exclusive to British houses. Each wire (the red 'live' for example) goes from the consumer unit to each socket in turn, and then back to the consumer unit, where the 'inward' and 'outward' ends are wired in together into the same terminal in the appropriate fuseholder. Each ring main is protected by its own fuse in the consumer unit. In addition, each appliance that it serves has a fuse in the plug, lessening the chance of actually blowing the main fuse and breaking the circuit. For this reason, the ring main is the safest and most widely used of all wiring systems

—have an earth wire connected to their outer casings and led indirectly to ground.

This is so that, if a live wire makes contact with the casing, the electricity will follow the path of least resistance to the ground. That is, it will flow through the earth wire instead of the person's body. At the same time, a live wire coming into contact with earthed metal-work will result in a large current flow that will blow the fuse.

The electricity flows from the live wire in this way because it is trying to reach the neutral—which is connected to earth back at the electricity board transformer. This system has been found to be the safest way of disposing of unwanted current.

## Fuses

A fuse is a deliberately weak link in the wiring, thinner than the wires on either side. If an overload occurs, the fuse wire melts and cuts off the current before the heat from the overloaded circuit can damage any equipment or actually cause a fire.

Fuses should always be of the nearest available size above the amperage of the appliance or circuit that they protect. Most electrical appliances have their wattage marked on a small plate fixed to the back or base of the unit. So, for an appliance connected to a ring main, you can use the formula above to find the amp rating and hence the correct fuse

that should be inserted in the electrical appliance's plug.

For example, say an electric fire has a rating of 3 kilowatts and the voltage of the mains is 240 volts. The current taken by the fire is found by dividing the watts—3,000—by the volts—240—which gives a result of 12.5 amps. Therefore, the fire should be protected with a 13 amp fuse, which is the nearest higher size of fuse available.

In Britain, it is recommended practice to use 3 amp cartridge fuses, colour coded red, for all appliances rated up to 720 watts, and 13 amp fuses, colour coded brown, for all the other appliances up to a maximum electrical rating of 3 kilowatts.

Most plugs come fitted with 13 amp fuses, the largest available size. But some appliances can be damaged by a current of less than 13 amps. So it pays to use the formula and check that the plugs on appliances are fitted with the correct size of fuse.

**F.** Types of fuse holder available. 1: Bridge wire fuse holder. 2: Cartridge fuse holder. 3: In a protected wire fuse holder, the wire run all the way through a tube. 4: The wire in this type of holder runs right across an asbestos mat.

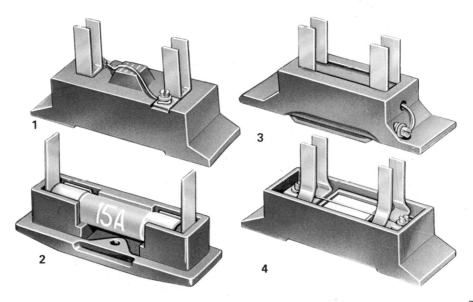

# Mend a fuse

There are three main types of circuit fuse: wire fuses, cartridge fuses and circuit breakers. It is important to know which type you have and to keep a supply of spare fuse wire or cartridges. Circuit breakers need no spares as they are switches which shut off if the circuit is overloaded; you will need, however, to rectify the fault.

Most fuse boxes are covered by a plate which either clips on or screws into place. **Always turn off the mains switch before removing the plate or touching any fuse.**

With the plate removed you will see a row of fuse carriers. Some are colour coded on the back: white for 5 amp lighting circuits, blue for 15 amp heating circuits and red for 30 amp power socket circuits.

Take out the first fuse—the holders simply pull out and clip back into place—then replace the cover and turn the mains switch back on.

Check each circuit until you find the one that has stopped working.

When a fuse blows, the first thing to do is to discover the cause and rectify it. If you suspect that the failure is due to a faulty appliance, unplug it and do not use it again until it has been mended.

To mend a wire fuse, loosen the screws and discard the broken wire. Cut a new length of wire of the correct amperage rating. Wrap the ends of the wire around the screws in a clockwise direction so that when you retighten the screws the wire is not dislodged. Finally, replace the holder and fuse box cover and switch the power back on.

# Wire a plug

**G.** Secure the flex in the cord grip by tightening its fixing screws. Strip the insulation from the end of the three wires, baring only enough wire to wrap safely around each terminal. Twist the strands and form a loop. Remove the plug cover by unscrewing the large screw between the pins to reveal the three terminals. The terminal at the top connects to the green and yellow earth wire. The brown live wire connects via the fuse to the live pin on the right and the blue neutral wire to the neutral terminal on the left. Some older appliances are coloured: green, for earth, red for live and black for neutral. Loosen the cord grip screws at the base of the plug. Remove the wire sheathing about 60mm and put under the grip and tighten the clamps. Cut the three wires and remove insulation. Twist the wires into strands, fix round each terminal and tighten the nut. Ensure that the right fuse is in place and then tighten the screw on the cover. Then test the plug to see if it is working correctly

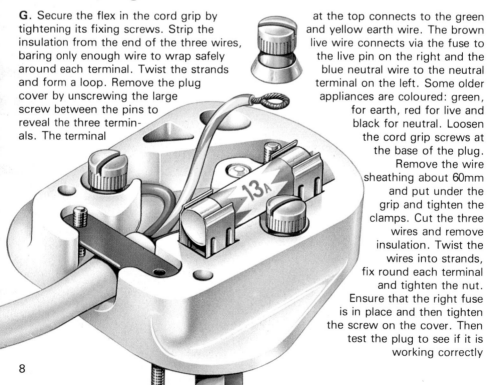

# Understanding the wiring

The bulk of the work in any electrical project is actually installing all the wiring. In Britain you can do your own wiring, provided the work is always carefully inspected by the supply authority in your district.

Electrical wiring in the home is made up of *fixed* wiring and *flexible* wiring. Fixed wiring, housed within the 'fabric' of the home, carries electrical current from the consumer unit (main fuse box) to fixed outlets such as sockets and lights. Flexible wiring provides the final link from a socket to an electrical appliance, or from a ceiling rose to a lampholder.

### Electrical cable

Fixed wiring consists of *cable*. This is made up of individual wires, or *conductors*, which carry the current, and *insulation* to prevent the current from leaking. In new wiring, the live and neutral conductors are usually insulated separately in colour-coded plastic sheaths then laid together with a bare earth wire in a common, outer sheath.

In some older installations, each conductor runs separately within its own inner, colour-coded and outer sheaths. In others the live and neutral conductors are housed in the same outer sheath but the earth insulation runs separately.

In **Britain**, the colour coding for cables is: red for live, black for neutral, and green/yellow striped for earth where this is insulated.

Modern cable is insulated with PVC which has an indefinite life and is impervious to damp and most common chemicals. Older installations may have been wired with rubber-insulated cable. This has a life of only about 30 years, after which it may begin to break up and become a potential danger. If your wiring is of this type, do not attempt to extend it, but replace it with the PVC type.

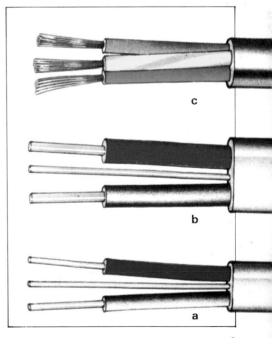

**A.** Some types of flex and cable that are in common usage at the present time in the UK. **(a)** Twin and earth cable used for the low amperage lighting circuits. Red is live, black is usually neutral, but might be live if connected to a light switch. **(b)** The same sort of cable but larger and used particularly for ring mains which take higher amperage. **(c)** Flex—commonly used for connecting plugs on appliances. The colour coding is different

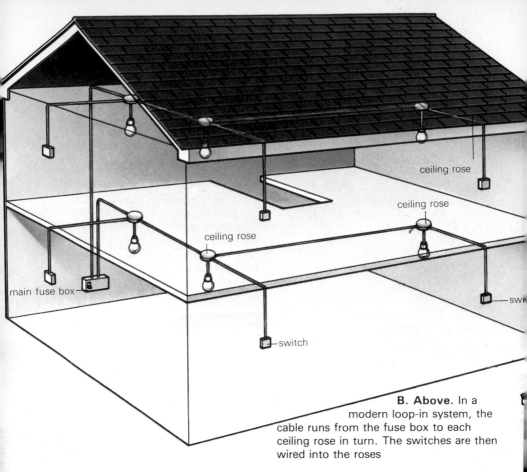

ceiling rose

ceiling rose

ceiling rose

main fuse box

sw...

switch

**B. Above.** In a modern loop-in system, the cable runs from the fuse box to each ceiling rose in turn. The switches are then wired into the roses

Fixed wiring runs around the home hidden beneath floorboards and buried in walls. When recessed in solid plaster, the cable is protected by a length of plastic or metal tube called a *conduit*. Beneath floorboards, the cable can run freely along the sides of, or through holes bored in, the floor joists.

When laid beneath floorboards, the cable should really be quite slack, but well supported—either by lying on the ceiling of the floor below, or by being carefully secured in place with strong cable clips.

### Electrical flex

The conductors in flexible wiring, or *flex*, are made up of a number of thin wires. This enables them to stand up to re-

peated twisting and coiling, as occurs when the flex is wrapped around an unused appliance. But though flex is strong along its length, it should never be strained at the ends. Never pull a plug out of a socket by the flex or you may strain the terminals and pull the wires loose, making the plug and flex potentially very dangerous.

In **Britain**, the conductors in three-core flex are colour coded brown for live, blue for neutral, green and yellow for earth. Older appliances, of which there may still be several in existence, may have flex with the same colour coding as

**Right:** In a junction-box lighting circuit, each ceiling rose and switch is wired to a junction box above the ceiling

cable: red (live), black (neutral) and green (earth).

The two-core flex for double-insulated appliances requiring no earth is not always colour coded. The conductors in a table lamp flex, for example, are often insulated in transparent plastic because on non-earthed appliances, it does not matter which conductor is actually connected to which terminal.

There are various thicknesses of flex conductor—appliances of high wattage ratings requiring thicker conductors than the ones which have a lower rating.

If you need to lengthen a flex for any reason, make sure that the new length is of the same type as the existing flex and use a factory-made connector of the correct amp rating to connect the two. Remember never to use insulating tape to join the conductors together.

## Lighting circuits

Older houses often have *junction-box* lighting circuits. In this system, the cable runs from the fuse box to junction boxes above the ceiling. Separate cables then run from the junction boxes to ceiling roses and light switches. You should not add a light to a junction-box circuit without first seeking expert electrical advice.

In the modern *loop-in* system the wiring is continuous, running from the fuse box to each ceiling rose in turn. The switches are wired directly to the roses. A light controlled by its own switch can be added to a loop-in system by wiring an extension from the circuit cable running into an existing ceiling rose.

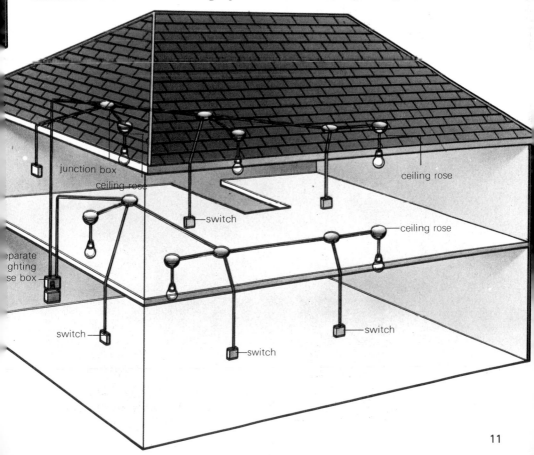

junction box

ceiling rose

ceiling rose

switch

ceiling rose

separate lighting fuse box

switch

switch

switch

# An extra light in the ceiling

Installing an extra light connected to an existing one, and controlled by the same switch, is a straightforward project.

The main items you need are a lampholder and a new ceiling rose. For connecting these two, buy 1mm² flex. If the lampholder you plan to use is brass, it will have to be earthed, so buy three-core flex. Otherwise buy two-core. For connecting the new ceiling rose to the old one, buy 1mm² twin-with-earth cable, allowing about 0.5m extra. Also buy a short length of 2mm green/yellow PVC sleeving to insulate each earth wire.

Decide where you want the light and drill a hole in the ceiling.

From the floor above, locate the hole and the existing ceiling rose. Enlarge the hole with a 13mm bit.

To mount the new ceiling rose base, a piece of 150mm × 25mm timber is fitted between the joists over the hole. Measure the distance between one of the joists and the hole and transfer the measurement to the piece of board. Drill a 13mm hole in the board, fit it over the hole in the ceiling and attach it with angle brackets to the joists on either side. You can now fix the rose base to the ceiling below.

Go back into the ceiling and run a length of cable from the existing light's ceiling rose to the new rose. If the cable route is parallel with the joists the cable can lie unclipped between them. If it runs at right angles to joists which are carrying floorboards, however, you will have to drill holes through the joists. Drill these at least 50mm from the tops of the joists to prevent damage from nails.

Next, prepare the cable for connection. First slit it for about 50mm from the end by sliding the blade of a handyman's knife between the live wire and the bare earth wire. With the sheathing removed

**Left:** An extra light can be readily fitted to a ceiling to bring a gloomy, dull corner of a room to life

for about 50mm (fig. 2), strip about 6mm of insulation from each wire.

## Wiring the new ceiling rose
Return to the floor below and prepare both ends of the flex that will run from the ceiling rose to the lampholder. Remove about 75mm of sheathing from the end to be connected to the ceiling rose and 50mm from the end for the lampholder. Sleeve the bare earth wire of the new cable (fig. 2) and connect the cable and the flex to the ceiling rose. It does not matter which of the ceiling rose terminals you use as long as you group the wires correctly in the same terminal block—the two lives (red cable and brown flex) together; the two neutrals (black cable and blue flex) together; and both earth wires together if your flex has them.

Tighten all the terminal screws and hook the flex wires over the two anchor pieces in the base of the ceiling rose. Slip the ceiling rose cover up over the flex and screw it onto the base. Then connect the lampholder to the other end of the flex, again hooking the wires over the anchor pieces and again checking the terminals.

## Wiring-in the extension
Before wiring-in the extension, you need to isolate the electric circuit you plan to work on. To do this, turn on the light to which the extension is to be made, and keep pulling fuses out of the consumer unit until the light goes off. (Turn off the power at the main switch as you withdraw or replace each fuse.) Once you have found and removed the fuse for the circuit you want to work on you can turn the main switch on again. This allows you, if you need light during the wiring process, to plug a standard lamp into a wall socket.

Since both lights are to be operated by the same switch, they are connected to the same terminals in the lighting circuit.

So the first thing to do is to identify the terminals to which the **flex** of the existing light pendant is connected. These are the terminals to which the live and neutral wires of the new cable must also be connected.

If the existing pendant flex has coloured conductor wires, wire the red live wire of the new cable to the same terminal as the brown flex wire of the old light pendant. Similarly, wire the black neutral wire of the new cable to the same terminal as the blue flex wire.

If the existing flex is not colour-coded, you cannot tell which side is the live. Your new cable must then be connected to the same terminals as the **old flex**, and not to any other terminal.

In either case, you may find you have to push one old wire and one new one into the same terminal hole.

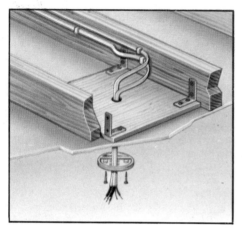

**1** Drill a hole in a board and fit it. The cables go into the hole and the rose

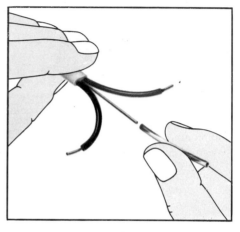

**2** Before connecting a cable, sleeve the earth wire with PVC sleeving

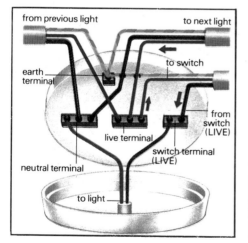

**3** In a modern rose, identify the groups of terminals

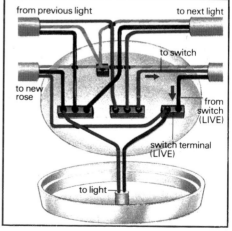

**4** Connect the cable for the new rose to the terminals

# Persistent fuse blowing

A circuit fuse is relatively simple to mend, but when a fuse continues to blow each time you replace it, either the circuit is overloaded—in which case you should switch off some appliances—or there is a serious fault somewhere along it which must be located and rectified before the circuit will function again. On no account must you replace the blown fuse with a length of wire or any other bridge, such as a nail. To do so would be tantamount to lighting a fire.

*Note:* Never work on a circuit until you are certain that it is not live.

Having a thorough understanding of the theory of fuses and the faults which cause them to blow will help you to maintain the electrical circuits around the home. And even if you do not intend to carry out the repair work yourself, being able to locate the area of a fault will help to save on the cost of repair.

## Why fuses blow

A fuse is a deliberately weak link included in the wiring of a circuit. If a surge of current occurs in the circuit, caused by a wiring fault of some kind or by overloading, the thin fuse wire is melted by the resulting extra heat generated by the current surge.

Fuses often blow because two wires in the circuit are in contact with one another. If the live and the neutral wires make contact, this is called a short circuit; when the live wire touches the earth it is called a line/earth fault or a short to earth. Or the live wire may be in contact with earthed metalwork —such as the mounting box of a flush-mounted light switch—to which the earthing core is always attached via a

screw-type earth terminal.

Although a fuse is a 'weak' link in the wiring, it requires quite a large amount of current before it blows. For example, a cartridge fuse requires a current of one and a half times its current rating before it melts, and a wire fuse may take a current of twice its rating.

But when a short circuit occurs, the resulting current surge is enormous. This is also the case with a line/earth fault—if the earthing is in good condition. If the earthing is faulty, there may be insufficient current to blow the fuse, in which case the fault will remain undetected and a potential fire hazard—the earth return will heat up due to the high resistance it meets.

A fault in an electrical appliance is unlikely to keep blowing the circuit fuse, if the circuit is protected by a cartridge

**1** This type of protected wire fuse holder has a window to let you see if the wire is broken. Cut a length of wire of the same amperage and fix it in place

**2** In the case of a blowing fuse in a lighting circuit, replace the fuse then test each light. Start at the lampholder

**3** Check that the wires in the rose are intact and that there is no contact between the earth and a live terminal

fuse in the appliance's plug as in UK 13 amp ring main circuits. But a circuit fuse may blow if the circuit is heavily overloaded—drawing far too much current.

**Miniature circuit breakers**
All the faults and checks described below apply equally whether your consumer unit is fitted with wire or cartridge fuses, or with the modern miniature circuit breakers. A miniature circuit breaker (MCB) is a single-pole switch which is automatically cut off when excessive current caused by a fault flows right through the circuit.

The principal differences between MCBs and normal fuses are that they require less current to shut them off than is needed to blow a fuse of the same current rating, and they operate more quickly. When a fault in the circuit persists, the circuit breaker trips immediately an attempt is made to switch it on.

**Cable faults**
If a circuit fuse continues to blow each time it is replaced, a possible cause is that two wires are in contact with each other somewhere along the cable of the

particular circuit in question.

If the wiring in your home is old, persistent fuse blowing may just be an indication that the wiring needs replacing altogether.

Trying to locate a specific fault on a relatively recent cable is a tedious job which is best left to an expert using special test equipment.

Cables are often damaged in the course of alterations to a home, so begin by checking the wiring around the site of any recent work.

Also check any recently installed wiring: you may have disturbed the old when running additional cable to new lights or socket outlets, or you may have failed to make proper connections to the new wiring.

**Lighting circuits**
If the main fuse of a lighting circuit keeps blowing, turn off all the light switches fed by that circuit, shut off the electricity supply at the mains then replace the fuse.

Turn on the mainswitch, then switch on each light switch in turn. When the fuse blows, you will have found the part of the circuit in which the fault lies. Now you must track it down.

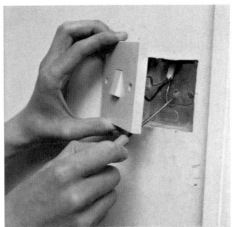

**4** If necessary, try to inspect the under-floor boxes for clues such as a smoky discoloration or melted insulation

**5** A typical source of trouble is an unsheathed earth wire meeting a live terminal behind the switch plate

The first thing to check is the flexible wiring which connects the lampholder to the ceiling rose. This may be worn or damaged, particularly if it is of the obsolete, twisted twin type. Once more, turn off the electricity supply and remove the relevant fuse holder. At the light, unscrew the lampholder to check the condition of the flex and make sure that the cores are securely connected to the terminals. If necessary, renew the faulty flex.

Now check the wiring in the ceiling rose by unscrewing the cover from the base which is fixed to the ceiling. A common problem here is that the earth wires are left unsheathed and make contact with one of the live terminals in the rose. If you find that this is the case, disconnect the wires from the earthing terminal, slip lengths of green and yellow PVC sleeving over them—leaving about 6mm of bare wire protruding—and reconnect them.

Where a bare earth wire is not the problem, check the condition of the remaining wires. If the insulation of these is all intact and they are connected tightly to the correct terminals, replace the rose cover and turn your attention to the light switch itself.

Remove the cover plate of the switch and check the wiring. The most likely fault is, again, that the earth wire is bare and in contact with the live terminal. But it may be that the fixing screws of the cover plate have penetrated the insulation of one of the wires and that, with a flush-mounted switch, a section of live wire is in contact with the earthed metal box.

If it is the live return wire that is damaged in this way, the fuse will blow only when the switch is turned on; but if it is the live feed wire which is damaged, the fuse will blow whether it is on or off. The latter fault is easily recognized by the burnt insulation and smoke marks around the damaged area.

Where the area of damage is slight, you can make do by firmly wrapping some insulating tape around the bare section then laying the wires carefully back into the box so that the screws will not interfere with them. But if the damage is particularly bad—such as where a wire has almost been severed—the length of cable must be replaced.

If, after examining the lampholder, ceiling rose, switch and any accessible

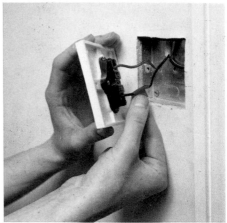

**6** The best way to insulate the bare insulation wire is to disconnect it then slip on a suitable length of green and yellow PVC sleeving

**7** In the case of slight damage to the neutral or live wires, bind the affected portion tightly with insulating tape and then refit the switch

cable you are still unable to find the fault, call in expert help.

## Power circuits

When the circuit fuse of a ring main circuit continues to blow, the fault is unlikely to be in one of the portable appliances plugged into the circuit: when these are faulty, the cartridge fuse in the plug will blow leaving the circuit fuse intact. However, before you start work on locating the fault, unplug all appliances and check that the fuse in each plug is of the correct amp rating.

On a ring main, the next step is to check the 30 amp main fuse. Very occasionally, when the circuit is already loaded to near its capacity, a fault on a small appliance may cause it to blow.

Other than an overload or a damaged circuit cable, the most likely fault in a ring main circuit is in the mounting box behind one of the socket outlets. Turn off the electricity supply at the mains and examine each socket in turn.

Unscrew the cover plate of the first socket and examine the wiring attached to the terminals on the back: the likely faults are similar to those that are found

in lighting switches.

Earth wires are often left uninsulated and therefore can easily make contact with the live terminal. This is particularly likely on a socket outlet as the earthing core is connected to a terminal on the back of the socket plate, rather than to one on the box, and can therefore be bent into a dangerous position. Cover with lengths of green and yellow PVC sleeving, then check the insulation of the live and neutral wires. These sometimes perish, if the terminals are not tightened properly or where a cheap—or faulty—plug or adaptor has been used in the socket and has overheated. Alternatively, the insulation may have been pierced by the socket's fixing screws. Deal with this problem as described above and, if necessary, use shorter screws to fix the socket plate into place.

When you have checked the first socket, replace the cover plate and move on to the next. Even if you think you have found and rectified the fault, it is worthwhile checking the remaining socket outlets.

If you do not find anything wrong with any of the sockets, the fault probably lies

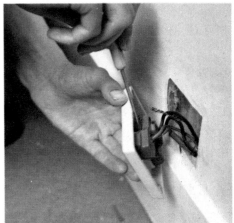

**8** In the case of a ring main circuit, it is necessary to check each socket in turn. A common fault is a bare earth wire touching a live wire

**9** Undo the bare earth wire and refit the live wire to the live terminal. Then sheath the earth wire with PVC sleeving and reconnect to the socket

somewhere along the cable of the circuit, so it is best to call in expert assistance, such as a qualified electrician.

### Cooker circuits

Because of the large amount of electricity it consumes, a free-standing electric cooker is always connected on a separate circuit protected by its own fuse in the main fuse box. The appliance is connected to its circuit by a special cooker control unit, which contains a switch and sometimes includes a separately controlled socket outlet. Neither the cooker nor its control unit contain a fuse, so a persistently blowing circuit fuse usually indicates a fault in either the control unit or in the appliance itself.

To find out whether the fault is in the unit or in the cooker itself, turn off the control switch, replace the circuit fuse with the relevant size of fuse wire or cartridge and turn on the power. If the fuse immediately blows again, the fault lies in the control unit or in the cable from the fuse board; with the power turned off, remove the unit's faceplate and inspect the wiring for damage as decribed above. If the fuse only blows when the cooker control switch is in the 'on' position, the fault is in the cooker itself and you should call in expert assistance to locate the fault.

### Immersion heaters

An immersion heater is usually supplied directly from its own circuit fuse with no other fuse intervening. When this circuit fuse blows, the fault is most likely to be in the immersion heater itself and therefore requires expert attention.

### Other circuits

Tracing faults on other sorts of circuit follows much the same methods as described above. First switch off at the mains, then unplug or disconnect all appliances and switch off lights on the faulty circuit. Switch on the mains, and carefully re-connect all appliances and switch on lights one by one until you find what causes the fuse to blow. Then check out the appliance or relevant part of the circuit, following the details above.

Whatever repairs you make to the fuse-box, sockets or wiring, be sure to turn off the electricity supply at the mains switch before starting work.

# How to install sockets

Today, the average home is equipped with a far greater number of electrical appliances than was the case a few years ago. And if many of these appliances are in use at the same time, there may not be enough sockets.

## Socket outlets

In the UK, the sockets that have three rectangular holes to accept the pins of 13 amp plugs are used on ring main circuits and on some partially modernized radial circuits. Socket outlets with round holes for 2 amp, 5 amp and 15 amp plugs are used only on radial circuits and usually indicate that the circuit is over 30 years old.

Modern socket outlets can be flush- or surface-mounted. The flush type is screwed onto a metal box which houses the cables and is recessed into the wall. For surface mounting, the same sort of socket is used, but this time screwed to a plastic box which is fixed to the wall surface.

Socket cover plates and, in the case of surface-mounted sockets, the box as well, are usually made of white plastic. But for installations in places like garages where outlets have to be more durable, sockets with metal cover plates and boxes are available.

In the UK, regulations require the live and neutral holes of 13 amp sockets to be fitted with protective shutters to prevent people (children especially) from poking metal objects inside with possibly fatal results. Most sockets also have a built-in switch to minimize the danger of touching live parts when you insert or remove a plug. Some switched sockets include a neon indicator light to show when the

socket is on. Switches are usually single-pole, cutting off the supply in the live wire only. This is usually sufficient: to totally isolate an appliance, remove the plug.

In a bathroom, where the presence of water increases the risk of electric shocks, the only sockets that can be installed are those specially designed for electric razors.

## Plug adaptors

In rooms where there are too few sockets to go round, or where appliances are too far from free sockets, plug adaptors—sometimes called socket adaptors—are often used to plug two or three appliances into the same socket.

A two-way adaptor with a fuse of the correct size is satisfactory for temporarily connecting low wattage appliances, such as table lamps or the hi-fi. But it is not advisable to use an adaptor for long periods or to plug in a high wattage appliance, such as a bar heater. By far the best approach is to add extra sockets.

## Adding socket outlets

If a room has an inadequate number of socket outlets and you have a ring main circuit, you can add extra ones without too much difficulty.

A ring circuit can have an unlimited number of socket outlets and, ideally, each room should have at least four—more in a kitchen. The circuit should serve a floor area of not more than 100m$^2$, which is more than the area of an average two-storey house. So, if you decide to install extra sockets, there is no limit to the number you can add as long

If you are working in an area of good natural light, turn off the electricity supply at the mains. If not, isolate the supply by removing the relevant circuit fuse and leave the lighting circuits functioning.

You must now find out whether or not your chosen socket is suitable for conversion. If it is on the main circuit, the socket can be converted without any problems. But if it is on a spur, no more outlets can be added to the spur.

To check the position of the socket in the circuit, unscrew the cover plate, ease it from the wall and examine the wiring. Two sets of wires connected to the plate suggests that the socket is probably not a spur. To make quite sure, examine the wiring in the nearest sockets on either side. If either of these has one set, or three sets of wires, the socket is on a spur and should not be converted. If the selected socket has three sets of wires, it is supplying a spur already and so cannot be used.

When you have satisfied yourself that the socket outlet is suitable, undo the terminal screws holding the cable cores into the plate and gently remove the cores inside. If the live, neutral and earth cores are twisted together, untwist them and then undo the mounting screws holding the metal box into its recess. Prise the box from the recess with a screwdriver or an old chisel.

To house the new, twin socket box, the recess must be extended. Mark the position on the wall and cut out the plaster and brickwork to the depth of the new box with a hammer and bolster. Knock out the punched holes in the box to accept the cables, feed these through, and position and screw the box into place using wall plugs. Twist the wires together again and wire up the twin cover plate as shown in fig. E. Screw the plate on to the box, switch on the power and test the socket.

The above procedure also applies to fitting a surface-mounted twin socket, though in this case no recess is needed—the box simply screws on to the wall.

**A.** Wiring up a single socket. Strip about 20mm insulation from the cores and then connect to the terminals

as they do not extend the circuit beyond the 100m² maximum.

Sockets are almost always mounted on a wall and should be positioned at a minimum height of 150mm above the floor level, or the working surface in a kitchen.

Though new sockets can be installed directly from the ring, it is often easier to wire it on a spur—an extension taken from the back of an existing socket.

Each existing socket outlet, or double outlet, can supply only one extra outlet—one single or one double socket.

## Single into twin socket

An even easier method of adding sockets is by converting single socket outlets into double ones. Where single sockets have been installed, the number of outlets in a room can be doubled, though none will be in new positions.

# A spur from the ring main

Running a spur from an existing socket means that you can place the new socket almost anywhere you like.

To wire the spur, you need a sufficient length of 2.5mm² cable 'twin with earth' to stretch from the existing socket to the site of the new one. You also need oval PVC conduit with securing clips and about 1m of green and yellow PVC sleeving. Choose as your source for the spur a socket as close to the proposed site as possible.

Before starting work, isolate the supply. Unscrew the cover of a possible socket and carefully compare the wiring. If a spur has already been taken from it or the socket itself is on a spur, it is not suitable. Unscrew a suitable socket and remove and untwist the wires. Prise the box away from its recess and knock out the relevant punched holes.

Hold the new box in position on the wall and draw around it to mark out its recess. Using a straight edge as a guide, draw two parallel lines—25mm apart—

between the new position and the existing recess, for the cable chase. Next cut the new recess and the chase with a hammer and bolster. The chase should be about 6mm deeper than the thickness of the conduit.

Knock out one of the punched holes in the new box and install it in its recess. Refit the box of the other socket as well, then cut the conduit to length so that it will protrude about 10mm into each box when installed in the chase. Fit the conduit, secure it and make good the plaster.

Wait until the plaster is dry then push the cable through the conduit so that about 200mm of cable protrude into each box, then remove the outer sheathing back to the edge of the box at both ends. Strip about 20mm of insulation from the live and neutral cores and sleeve the earth wires with lengths of green and yellow PVC sleeving, leaving about 20mm of bare wire protruding. Wire up the new socket cover plate as shown in

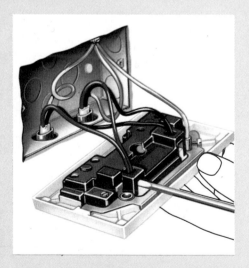

**B.** Unscrew the cover of an existing socket to check that it is suitable for connecting to a spur

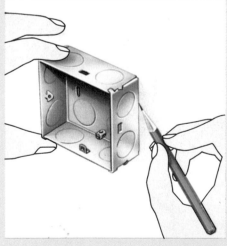

**C.** Mark the position for the new spur socket, then cut the recess for the box and the cable chase

fig. A and screw the plate in place.

Returning to the other box, connect the three red wires together and the three black wires together. Sleeve the earth wires if necessary, then twist together as shown in fig. F. Wire the plate up, carefully as shown in fig. F. Then screw it back on to the wall. Finally, switch back on at the main fusebox and plug an appliance into the new socket to check that it works correctly. Recheck wiring if necessary.

**D.** Push a cable through the conduit from the original box. Then remove the outer sheathing

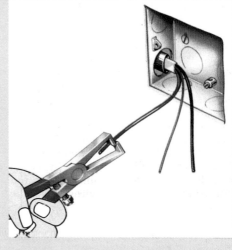

**E.** With the sheathing removed back to the edge of the box, bare the ends of the wires with wire strippers

**F.** With older cables, using separate strands, twist the ends of each group of wires firmly together

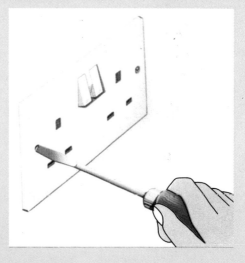

**G.** Wire up the cover plate and screw it back into place on its mounting box. Then test the new socket

# Light switches

Having light available at the flick of a switch is something we have all come to take for granted. But there is more to domestic switching circuitry than the simple on/off device. Innovations like two-way switching and dimmer switches make lighting more flexible.

## Lighting switches

Switches work by interrupting the flow of electricity through wires connecting the mains supply to the light itself. Most switches are *single-pole*—they make or break the supply passing through only one wire. It is important that this is the live wire of a circuit so that the light is isolated from the live supply when the switch is off. In no circumstances should a single-pole switch be inserted into the neutral pole; if it were, the light fitting would be live even when the switch was in the off position.

The type of switch usually installed in UK homes is an all-insulated unit with rocker action. This has a plastic or metal cover plate which is usually part of the switchgear. For surface mounting, the switch can be screwed to a plastic box which is fixed to the wall surface; for flush mounting, it can be screwed to a recessed metal box.

Pull-cord switches are used in bathrooms and kitchens where it is particularly important that people with wet hands cannot directly touch electrical fittings.

*Note:* Always remember *never* work on a circuit until you are certain that it is not live.

## Two-way switching

It is often convenient to be able to switch on a light at either of two locations. Ordinary switches cannot do this independently of each other—you can always switch the light off at either switch, but you cannot always switch it on. If you want to switch at two places independently, then you need two-way switches.

An ordinary one-way switch has two terminals, one for the live feed and one for the live return, but a two-way switch needs three terminals, marked in the UK, *common*, *L1* and *L2*. In the basic two-way switching circuit, the switch drop is linked to the L1 and L2 terminals of the first switch, and its three terminals are then linked to the corresponding three

**A.** A cross-section through a rocker switch. This is the switch most commonly used in British houses. It is an all-insulated unit with a rocker action

terminals of the second two-way switch using three-core and earth cable.

## Dimmer switches

As an alternative to a simple on/off switch, a dimmer switch greatly increases finger-tip control.

A dimmer switch is an electronic device, the main components of which are a semi-conductor called a *triac* and a printed circuit. Modern dimmer switches also contain a 2 amp fuse to protect the triac from the surge in current when a light bulb blows.

By rotating the knob of the dimmer, you can reduce the intensity of the light from the full, normal strength to any lower level: an effect which is achieved by blocking out part of the incoming current.

There are various types of dimmer switch on the market, the simplest and cheapest of which have a rotary dial which switches the light on and also controls the brightness. But this means that each time you switch on, you have to reset the desired level of illumination. Another type gets round the problem by having a normal rocker on/off switch alongside a rotary dimming wheel and a third type has a single knob with push/on, push/off switching action.

A more recent development in dimmer switches is the 'touch' dimmer. This has no moving parts, but is fitted instead with two separate touch pads. A quick tap of the finger on the upper pad turns the light on and a continued gentle touch raises the level of brightness. Touching the lower pad decreases the light intensity, and a quick tap turns the light off.

When choosing dimmer switches, bear in mind that fluorescent lights require a special type and that changes must be made to the light circuitry.

## Multiple switches

If you want to control more than one light independently, then you will need, obviously, more than one switch. Although you can of course always have

separate switches mounted in their own boxes, it is neater and easier if the switch mechanisms are close together, sharing a mounting box.

In the UK, this is usually done by using multi-gang switches. Up to three separately-controlled switch mechanisms can be mounted together on a plate that covers the same area as a standard, single-gang switch. Four- and six-gang switches are also available. All these multi-gang switches are of the two-way type, but of course any two-way switch can be used on a simple one-way circuit. Use the common and L1 terminals.

## Damaged switches

To replace a damaged switch, turn off the electricity supply at the mains, remove the switchplate from its box and disconnect the wires attached to the terminals.

If the damaged switch is a two-way switch, note which wire goes to which terminal and be sure to replace it with a switch of a similar type. If more than one wire is connected to any one terminal, keep these joined together and treat them as one wire. Wire up the replacement switch in the same manner as the old one and screw the cover plate into place.

If you have a cord-operated switch that is sluggish in action, turn off the power, remove the cover and squirt aerosol lubricant into the mechanism. When a cord snaps or is pulled out of its socket, it is better to buy and fit a replacement cord.

If a dimmer switch fails, isolate the supply, remove the switchplate and check that the wiring is correct and intact. If it is, the problem is probably due to a current overload having damaged the triac or some other component. In this case, the dimmer will have to be returned to the manufacturer.

## One-way to two-way switching

Almost any one-way switched light can be converted simply and economically to a more convenient two-way system. For this you require two two-way switches:

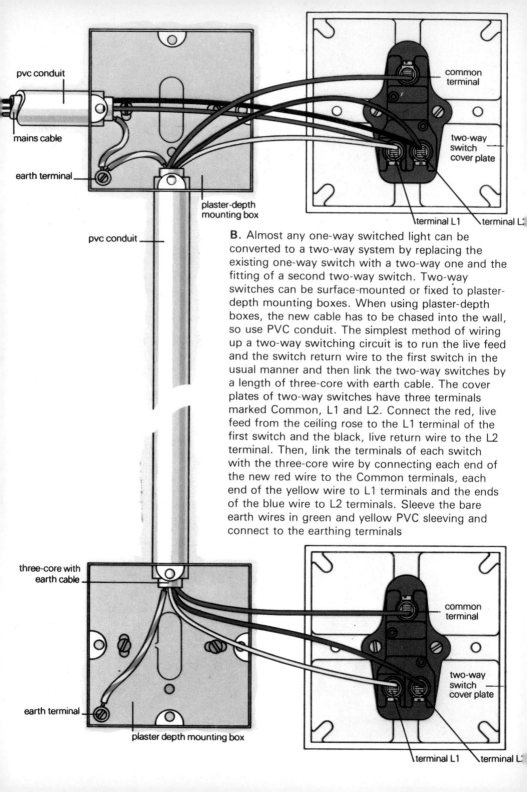

pvc conduit

mains cable

earth terminal

plaster-depth
mounting box

pvc conduit

common
terminal

two-way
switch
cover plate

terminal L1    terminal L2

**B.** Almost any one-way switched light can be
converted to a two-way system by replacing the
existing one-way switch with a two-way one and the
fitting of a second two-way switch. Two-way
switches can be surface-mounted or fixed to plaster-
depth mounting boxes. When using plaster-depth
boxes, the new cable has to be chased into the wall,
so use PVC conduit. The simplest method of wiring
up a two-way switching circuit is to run the live feed
and the switch return wire to the first switch in the
usual manner and then link the two-way switches by
a length of three-core with earth cable. The cover
plates of two-way switches have three terminals
marked Common, L1 and L2. Connect the red, live
feed from the ceiling rose to the L1 terminal of the
first switch and the black, live return wire to the L2
terminal. Then, link the terminals of each switch
with the three-core wire by connecting each end of
the new red wire to the Common terminals, each
end of the yellow wire to L1 terminals and the ends
of the blue wire to L2 terminals. Sleeve the bare
earth wires in green and yellow PVC sleeving and
connect to the earthing terminals

three-core with
earth cable

earth terminal

plaster depth mounting box

common
terminal

two-way
switch
cover plate

terminal L1    terminal L2

one to be fitted in place of the existing one-way switch and the other for fitting in your chosen new position.

Before you buy the new switches, turn off the electricity supply at the mains and remove the switchplate on the existing switch. If it has three terminals on the back marked as described above, it is a two-way switch wired for one-way operation and you need buy only one new two-way switch.

For mounting the wall switches you will need a mounting box—two, if you are replacing the existing switch with one of a different pattern. The boxes can be either flush- or surface-mounted.

Although switches can be wired in practice as shown in fig. A, this method is rarely used, and is particularly inconvenient when modifying existing wiring. The usual method makes use of special cable—1.0mm$^2$ three-core and earth cable. There are three insulated cores coloured red, yellow and blue, plus a bare earth wire. Buy enough to run from the existing switch position all the way to your additional switch.

You also need a length of green and yellow PVC sleeving for sheathing the ends of the bare earth wires and some red insulating tape to stick around the yellow and blue wires so that they are easily identified as live.

If you are installing two-way switching in a room with two doors, it is usual to place the switches near the doors so that you can chase the plaster out for the cable to run up the side of the architrave. If, on the other hand, you intend to run the new cable over the surface of the wall, the architrave can be used to secure the clipping. Better still use a box section conduit with a snap-on lid section: this can be stuck to the wall with contact adhesive. Box section conduit is not only safer than bare surface wiring but also looks a lot neater.

## Wiring a two-way switch

Begin by turning off the electricity supply at the mains, then remove the cover plate of the existing switch and unscrew the wires attached to the terminals. Next, prepare any cable chases and any recesses for boxes. If boxes are to be flush mounted, knock out one of the punched holes in the back for the cable and fit the box.

Where necessary, install your PVC conduit then run the new cable from the existing switch position to the new position, clipping it to the wall surface or feeding it through the conduit as necessary. Then make good any damaged plaster at this stage.

Remove about 150mm of outer sheathing from each end of the cable, leaving 12mm protruding into each box, then strip about 10mm of insulation from the end of each wire and double the ends over. Bind a short piece of red insulating tape around each yellow and blue wire, about 20mm from the end, and slip a length of green and yellow PVC sleeving over both bare earth wires and the earth wire of the original cable, if not already sleeved. If there is no red tape around the existing black insulating wire, put a piece on at this stage.

Now wire up the two switches as follows:
● At the original switch position, connect the earth wires to the box earth terminal
● Connect the original red wire and the new blue wire to the terminal marked L1
● Connect the existing black wire and the new yellow wire to the terminal marked L2
● Connect the new red wire to the 'Common' terminal
● At the new position, connect the red wire to the 'Common' terminal
● Connect the blue wire to the terminal marked L1
● Connect the yellow wire to the terminal marked L2
● Connect the earth wire to the box earth terminal.

Lay the wires neatly in the boxes and fix the switchplates in place with the screws provided. After you have turned on the power at the mains, the new switching arrangement can be tested.

# Fitting a dimmer switch

To replace a one-way switch with a standard dimmer, begin as always by turning off the power supply; then remove the cover plate of the existing switch and disconnect the two wires on the back. Try the dimmer switch plate in the wall box and arrange the wires so that they will not be trapped.

As the black wire carries the current back from the switch, and is therefore also live, it is best to clearly mark it as live with a piece of red insulating tape.

Now check that the wires fit properly into the terminal holes on the back of the dimmer switch plate. Some dimmers have terminals with holes that are much shallower than those of a normal switch. If this is the case, trim each wire to make sure that no bare wire is left protruding from the terminals (fig. 4).

Having made sure that the new dimmer fits neatly into the box, connect the two wires as for a normal switch,

following the instructions, or diagram.

If the switchplate of the dimmer is metal, it will have an earth terminal on the back. Make sure that this is connected to the box earth terminal by a short length of green and yellow PVC insulated wire (fig. 3).

Now fit the switch into place, making sure that no wires are trapped, and screw in the fixing screws. Switch the dial off if necessary. Turn the power on again and your new dimmer is ready.

If you want to replace a two-way switch with a dimmer, make sure that the type you choose for the job has three terminals on the back. Dimmers that incorporate a rocker switch alongside the dial or a push switch are the most suitable.

Touch dimmers and time lag dimmers will replace both one-way and two-way rocker switches. Make the connections according to the manufacturer's instructions.

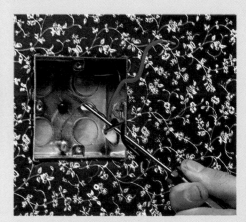

**1** To replace a one-way switch with a standard type of dimmer, first turn off the electricity supply at the mains and then unscrew the switch cover plate. With the cover of the existing switch completely removed from the mounting box, carefully unscrew the terminal screws so that you can easily free all the attached wires

**2** If you discover when you have managed to free the wires that the earth wire, which is connected up to the box terminal, is bare, loosen the terminal screw so that you can free the wire. You should then firmly sleeve it in a short length of green and yellow PVC sheathing for insulation purposes and to give the wire better protection

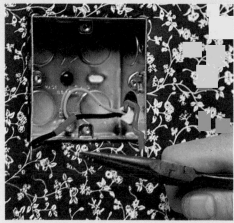

**3** Make sure when you sleeve the earth wire that about 6mm of bare wire is left protruding at the end. As the black wire in a switch is also live, it is best to highlight this fact, for any necessary future work, by carefully wrapping a piece of red insulating tape around it as marker for future reference

**4** If the terminal holes in the new dimmer are less deep than those existing in the switch, trim the wiring so that no bare end is left protruding. When you have trimmed both wires to length, connect up the switch following the detailed wiring instructions which will be given by the manufacturer

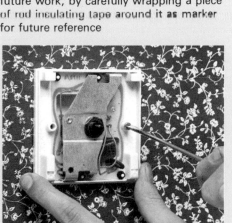

**5** Next, having connected up all the wiring on the switch you should use the mounting screws provided to actually fix the switch plate to the mounting box already on the wall. The last piece of work to do on this project is then to screw or clip the fixing cover, which houses the rotary dimmer switch control into position

**6** Now you should make sure that the control knob is fixed in the 'off' position. Then turn the electricity supply back on at the mains and rotate the switch back and forth to test out the performance of your new dimmer. You will then begin to appreciate the attractive and special effects achieved by dimmed or subdued lighting

# Time switches

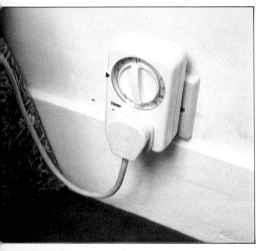

With fuel costs spiralling all the time, anything that enables you to control your electricity consumption is worth considering. Electric time switches offer a way of doing just that—particularly for heating and ventilating appliances.

A time switch can be fitted to almost any appliance and will automatically switch it on and off at preset times.

### Types of time switch

A time switch is quite simply a rotary switch—usually single pole—driven by a small electric clock. The switch has a dial which generally makes one revolution every 24 hours, although some models make one every week.

The dials are usually calibrated at

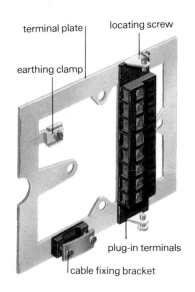

terminal plate | locating screw

earthing clamp

plug-in terminals

cable fixing bracket

**Above, top:** A variable time delay switch can be used to control small appliances such as electric blankets. **Above, bottom:** A time switch featuring a photo-electric cell is an easily fitted deterrent against burglars

intervals of 15 minutes so that the control periods can be selected with reasonable accuracy. Most units have two sets of tripping cams on the clock which provide two control periods every 24 hours, while some provide for several control periods but with a minimum interval between ON and OFF of about half an hour.

Some models of time switch contain a reserve battery to keep the clock going if the mains power supply is interrupted.

Once set for a programme of ON and OFF switching, a time switch continues with the programme until it is changed. However, most have a manual override switch allowing you to switch the appliance on and off at your own convenience.

Although time switches are usually wired to a circuit, several models plug into an ordinary socket or mains outlet. These models have their own socket into which, in turn, appliances can be plugged and, like other time switches, include a manual override.

Plug-in time switches have a maximum rating of about 3000 watts, while units that are plumbed into the mains have a variety of higher ratings. The usual rating is high enough to cover most requirements.

## Applications

A time switch can be used to control almost any appliance, but on no account should it ever be used to control a radiant electric fire: surprise switching could scorch an unsuspecting child or burn furniture and fittings, causing a fire hazard.

One circuit where a time switch is par-

**A. Below:** One type of time switch has separate supplies for switch and appliance, allowing the appliance to be isolated without actually stopping the clock

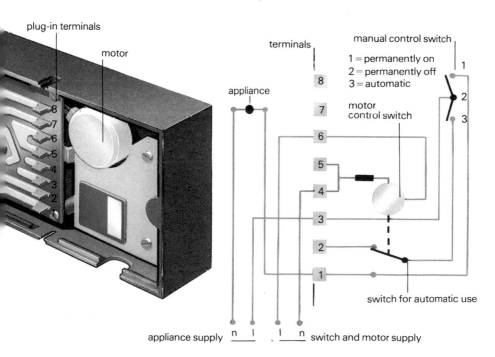

plug-in terminals

motor

terminals

appliance

manual control switch

1 = permanently on
2 = permanently off
3 = automatic

motor control switch

1
2
3

8
7
6
5
4
3
2
1

switch for automatic use

appliance supply   n l    l n   switch and motor supply

ticularly useful for energy-saving is the one supplying an immersion heater for electric hot water heating. You can programme the timer to switch on the heater about an hour before hot water is required (three hours for a bath) in the morning and evening.

Another useful place for a time switch is in the circuit supplying fixed electric heaters used as background heating (even when these have built-in thermostats). Among the heaters most suited to time switch control are tubular heaters, skirting heaters, and the oil-filled type of electric radiators.

The timer will usually be wired in the circuit supplying power to the heaters. So ensure no other appliances are fitted in the same circuit 'downstream' of the timer—otherwise these will be switched on and off in time with the heaters.

## Controlling storage heaters

If you wish to take advantage of the cheap off-peak rates offered by the local electricity boards in the UK, a storage heater controlled by a time switch is a sound investment. You can set the controls so that it draws electricity at the cheapest rate, and then emits heat throughout the day while it is switched off.

Although the electricity boards install storage heaters with their own circuit and consumer unit, you can install and run a single storage heater from a 13 amp socket using a plug-in time switch to turn it on and off. If you wish to install more than two heaters, however, it is best to supply each of them from a spur on the ring main with its own, wired-in time switch.

## Burglar deterrent switching

Lights left burning all night are just as likely to arouse the attentions of a would-be intruder as a house left in perpetual darkness. Time switches controlling table lamps in the bedrooms, kitchen and living room make excellent deterrents for this very reason, though the timers need resetting every few weeks to follow light-

ing-up times reasonably closely. Set the timers so that different rooms are lit up at different times up to about midnight.

## Installing a time switch

The first stage in installing a wired-in time switch is to find a suitable location for it. However, when doing so there are a few things you should bear in mind.

A time switch does not need to be next to the appliance—it can be placed in any convenient and accessible position: next to the consumer unit (fuse box), alongside the meter, in a cupboard. But if the appliance has a manual control switch, it is best to install the time switch between this and the consumer unit so that you can turn off the appliance manually without stopping (and having to re-set) the timer.

Another factor to consider is the layout of the wiring. If you are installing a new appliance, and are extending an existing circuit, then the time switch will need to be somewhere in this new run—look for a discreet but fairly accessible location.

Fitting a time switch in an existing circuit is often a simple matter of breaking into the circuit and connecting up the unit as described below. Where you have to run a new circuit to the appliance, installation details will depend on whether the new circuit forms an extension to a lighting circuit, a spur off a ring main, or a separate circuit. Make sure you use a timer of a sufficient current rating for the circuit you are connecting into, and that you use the right size cable.

Note: Make sure you never work on a circuit until you are certain that it is not live.

Like a light switch, the time switch itself must be partially dismantled before it can be fitted and wired; most time switches have a screw-on cover which must be removed to allow access to the terminals inside it. Remove this carefully, taking care not to damage the clock mechanism, and locate the holes in the casing for the cables, and the screw terminals for connecting the wires.

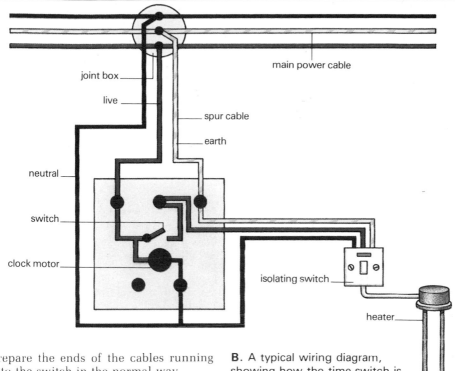

joint box

live

neutral

switch

clock motor

main power cable

spur cable

earth

isolating switch

heater

Prepare the ends of the cables running into the switch in the normal way.

The next step is to fix the unit to a wall, using screws and wall plugs, or to a convenient shelf near the consumer unit. Having done so, start connecting the wires from the supply and the appliance. The live wire from the supply is connected to one side of the clock/switch mechanism, the live wire to the appliance is connected to the other. The neutral wires may have a common terminal, as may the earth wires, so be sure to consult the manufacturer's wiring diagram and find out which is which (fig. A).

Sheath the bare earth cables before fitting them, then fit the remaining wires, tighten up the screw terminals, and replace the top cover. Set the timer to the switching periods you require, set the clock to the correct time, and switch on the supply.

### Thermostatic control

Thermostats serve a similar purpose to

**B.** A typical wiring diagram, showing how the time switch is fitted on a spur cable so that its operation does not affect other appliances in the home

time switches: they provide automatic control of your heating system, switching heaters on and off as they are required and maintaining a constant temperature so that no energy is wasted raising the temperature of a room to an unnecessarily high level.

Some heaters have a built-in thermostat that can be set to any temperature you require, but the majority do not. For these you can buy a unit similar to a plug-in time switch, which plugs into a socket outlet and into which the heater itself is plugged.

To achieve accurate control you should make sure that the unit is plugged into a socket well out of the way of draughts. But as with time switches, radiant electric fires should never be used with thermostats due to the risk of fire.

33

**1** To install a time switch in an immersion heater circuit, you should first isolate the circuit and then remove the cable clips securing the cable. Next, take the fixing plate off the time switch, and using a loop of the cable, find a suitable location for it, as close as possible to the isolating switch

**2** When you have found a suitable location, mark the screw hole positions. Drill the screw holes through the pencil marks. Use wall plugs if fixing the switch to plaster. Otherwise use wood screws of the correct size, secure the fixing plate of the time switch to the wall. Make sure that it is the right way up

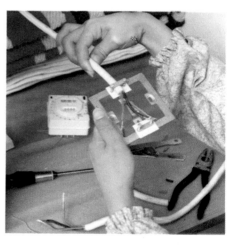

**3** Lay the loop of cable carefully over the fixing plate and, allowing 50mm for connections on each side, cut it in line with the middle of the plate. Then strip back the cable sheathing for about 50mm, and then you should strip the insulation on the wires inside down to a depth of about 10mm

**4** Now feed the unsheathed wires into the metal backing plate and then fix the cables using the cord grips, which are provided on each side of the plate. The earth wires on this switch have a common connection terminal. In this case twist the bared ends firmly together with the help of a pair of pliers

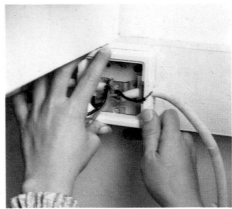

**5** When you have done this, fit the earth wires into the earth terminal on the fixing plate and then tighten up the terminal screw firmly. Now using the screws, which have been supplied in the kit, fit the backing plate to the fixing plate—first making sure that it is being fitted the right way round

**6** When the backing plate is fixed firmly in place, turn your attention to the next task which should be completed. The piece to be fitted next is the adaptor for the clock and the switch mechanism. This should simply be pushed firmly and securely into the correct place and just left there

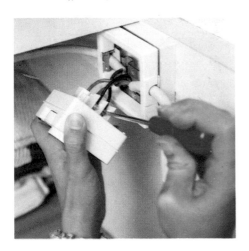

**7** Look out the manufacturer's wiring diagram for the timer and make sure you follow all the instructions carefully. Then connect up the live and neutral wires to their terminals on the back of the switch. Do not forget the neutral wires may have the same terminal as may the earth wires, so check the instructions first

**8** Having made sure you have sheathed the earth wires, you now need to tighten up the single screw which holds the switch mechanism in place. Then set the clock to the correct time and set the tripping pins to the switching periods you require. Then you can begin to test the timer to see that it works correctly

# Channelling electric cables

Few things are more unsightly and potentially dangerous than electric cables running across ceilings and down walls. Your first consideration when wiring sockets, switches or light fittings should always be to hide such cables safely and unobtrusively.

When a house is wired during its construction, cables are usually hidden from view in various ways—in chases or channels cut in masonry walls; behind the wall covering of timber-framed walls; hidden under the floor or above ceiling level.

New cables can be hidden in much the same way—by cutting chases in masonry walls; dropping them through the hollow centre to be found in most timber-framed walls; or by lifting floorboards and threading cables along or through joists.

An alternative, which can save a lot of redecoration, is to run the cables along the surface of walls or ceilings—but neatly hidden in plastic box-shaped channels called trunking.

## Planning wall cables

Cables channelled into walls are usually connected to wall switches or wall-mounted lights, but they are sometimes also used to carry power to socket outlets or to individual appliances such as cookers.

During the construction of new houses, wall-run cables are fitted into plastic conduits prior to being channelled into the wall. This keeps the cable in position during construction and offers some means of protection once the walls have been plastered.

But when you are channelling through walls that are already plastered you can use plastic conduit, plastic cover strip, or—even safer—galvanized steel cover strip.

Once a channel has been cut to the required depth, the cable is fed into it and then covered with protective capping. The work is completed by plastering the channel level with the existing wall surface.

When planning cables to run along walls, make sure that they are placed according to accepted practice so that anyone drilling into the wall at a later date can avoid them.

## Channelling wall cables

Before cutting out channels to accommodate the cables, carefully mark their proposed positions on the wall. Hold a long straightedge against the surface and draw two parallel lines across the wall, slightly more than the width of your conduit or capping apart.

Once the whole run has been completely marked out to your satisfaction, including the position of power points and switches, reposition the straightedge against the lines and run the blade of a handyman's knife along it. Try to cut through wall-coverings—if there are any —and into the top layer of plaster (fig. 1).

Once the channel has been cut along both sides, peel away any wall coverings from the centre until the plaster below is fully exposed. Then use a sharp bolster to cut first down the centre line, then the outside edges, of the channel until you have removed all the plaster.

The channel should be at least 20mm deep, and to achieve this you may have to cut into the brick or block work. Use an 18mm cold chisel, and be sure to wear

**1** When channelling cable through walls, mark all the proposed positions. Then place a straightedge along the marked out lines and run a handyman's knife along them to cut through the wallcovering. Peel and scrape away the paper until the plaster below it is fully exposed and ready to cut away

**2** With a sharp bolster cut first down the centre and then down each outside edge of the proposed channel. Continue to do this until you reach the brick or blockwork behind it. Since the channel needs to be at least 20mm deep you may need to use an 18mm cold chisel and hammer to cut into the masonry

**3** First screw the back of the protective channelling firmly into place using plugs drilled and fixed into the wall behind the recess. Then thread the cable into place making sure that it is all straight, does not have any kinks, and that it fits neatly into the backing part of the channelling

**4** Snap the front of the channelling on the backing to cover the cable and help protect it from damage. Secure the whole channel by spacing galvanized nails along both sides. Finally you should plaster the channel so that it is level with the existing wall. Use a straightedge to clear away any loose material

**5** Before channelling cable under floorboard level, mark its route in straight lines across the floorboards with a piece of chalk. Then raise all the marked-out floorboards using a bolster. Once the joists are fully exposed, mark the position of the intended run midway between the two adjacent floorboards

**6** Use a spade or flatbit attachment to drill the necessary holes. Make them all slightly larger than the cable—but they should be no wider than 25mm. If space between the joists is very cramped make more room for the drill by cutting the drill bit in half with a medium-toothed hacksaw

**7** Another alternative to the awkward problem of drilling holes in the joists is that you can actually fit a right-angle adaptor to the power drill. This particular attachment is very useful as it allows you to insert the drill and to work in comfort from a point above each of the joists you need to drill into

**8** Unkink the length of electrical cable and thread it through each drilled hole in turn. Take care that it does not become at all damaged or twisted in the process. When you replace each floorboard again, keep the nails well away from the chalked cable line you have previously marked on the floor surface.

safety glasses or goggles to protect your eyes from flying chips of masonry. Always angle the chisel in towards the centre, to avoid accidental damage to the rest of the wall.

Once all the channelling is complete, cut out chases for light switches and power points in the same way. Check the depth of each chase carefully to ensure that the relevant fitting can be mounted flush with the wall, then knock out the cable entry blanks nearest the channel feeding it and fix the fitting securely in position.

If you are using plastic conduit to protect the cable, fix it in the channel at this stage, using galvanized nails. Then thread the cable into position in the conduit and connect it to the fittings, but not to a power souce.

Then plaster over the top of the conduit using the same techniques employed to plaster a small hole. Make sure that the plaster is pushed hard into the channel, then place the straightedge across and move it up and down in a sawing motion to remove excess material and leave a smooth, flat finish.

Clear loose plaster from around the live terminals at each fitting, then leave the wall to dry for at least three to four hours before connecting the circuit to the mains and switching the power back on.

## Underfloor cables

Much of the cable used in house wiring is run in the space under a suspended ground floor or between the ceiling of a downstairs room and the floor of the room above. Here the cable is relatively safe, requires the minimum of fixings to hold it in place, and is protected from damage by the timbers around it. Where the cable has to pass across joists, you should feed it through holes drilled in them. These holes must be at least 50mm below floorboard level, and must not extend below the centre lines of the joists.

Plan where you want the cable to run, marking the floorboards with chalk if necessary. Try as much as possible to

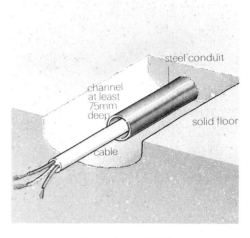

**A. Above:** Through a solid floor cut a 75mm deep channel using either a cold chisel or otherwise a power chasing tool

keep these marks in straight lines running across the joists so that you have to lift as few floorboards as possible (fig. 5).

With the cable route clearly planned, raise all of the marked floorboards and expose the joists below. In many cases the joists may already have been drilled to accommodate cables and if you notice a line of holes running near where you have lifted floorboards, use these to accommodate your own length of cable. But if no such holes exist, you will have to drill fresh ones.

Mark the positions of the holes on the joists so that they lie midway between the two adjacent floorboards.

Use either a flooring brace or a power drill, fitted with a 90° adaptor and a flat bit, to make the holes. If you do not have these tools, there should be enough space between the joists to insert a power drill fitted with a spade or flatbit cut in half. Always make the holes slightly larger than the cable so that you can feed it through without difficulty.

When you replace the floorboards, make sure that you keep the nails well away from the chalked cable line marked on the surface.

## Cables in the roof space

PVC sheathed cables run in the roof space to supply lights and switches in the rooms below. But unless the loft is converted into an extra room there is no need to drill holes in the ceiling joists to accommodate them. They can be run across the joists, fixed at intervals with cable clips, or alongside joists and rested on the ceiling.

However, where the roof is insulated with expanded polystyrene granules, protect the cable with plastic conduit fixed along the top of the joists. If the plasticizer contained in the PVC cable sheathing comes into contact with the granules, it eventually damages the cable itself, leading eventually to dangerous, bare wires in the roof space.

**B. Below**: A plastic conduit system provides you with all the straight sections,

## Skirting boards and architraves

If you have a room where the floor is solid, or is decorated with tiles or some other permanent floor covering, an alternative to cutting chases in the wall is to hide the cable behind skirting boards and architraves. Although this involves removing these features, the final result is neat and comparatively safe if it is done well.

Prise the skirting board and architrave away from the wall and then make sure that there is enough space to accommodate the cable once these have been replaced. If necessary, use a bolster or cold chisel to cut a shallow channel in the wall behind.

Then position the cable, pushing it deep into the recess behind the skirting board and into the gap between the architrave and the door frame. Then replace the skirting board and architrave,

angled adaptors and boxes for covering up any ugly exposed wiring

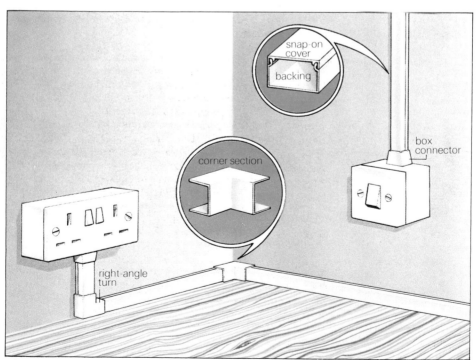

snap-on cover

backing

corner section

box connector

right-angle turn

making absolutely sure that none of the fixing nails are positioned near the cable run.

If the floor is of bare concrete, it may be more practical over short distances to channel straight through it. And although you can cut such a channel with a hammer and bolster, it is a great deal less work to hire a power chasing tool for the job.

Cables running through concrete must always be encased in steel conduit—available from electrical stores and builders' merchants—and the channels themselves must be at least 75mm deep. This may breach the floor's damp-proof membrane. To ensure its continuity, brush two coats of bitumen-based damp-proofing liquid into the chase.

After you have fed the cable through the conduit and laid the latter in position, make good the channelling with a mortar mix of one part cement to three of sharp sand with a little PVA bonding agent added.

## Using plastic trunking

Plastic trunking provides a means of safely channelling electric cable without either cutting into walls or lifting floorboards. The box-shaped channel runs across ceilings and can be used to accommodate any type of two or three core cable for lights, switches or power points.

The trunking is designed in two parts, the back being easy to fix in place while the front snaps off to allow the cable to be inserted. The system includes boxes for switches, socket outlets and fused connection units, and these, too, are fixed directly to the surface of the wall. Trunking can be screwed in place, or stuck with impact adhesive.

Fix the baseplates of switches and so on first, then fix the back part of the conduit. Lay the cable in place, make the electrical connections and snap on the covers. Finally, connect up the cable to the mains.

You may have some problem linking power from an existing socket to the new one. If the existing socket is directly below the new outlet, simply drop a length of cable down the cavity to where you want it. If the existing socket is some distance away, it is best to drop the cable down the cavity and then lead it behind the skirting board.

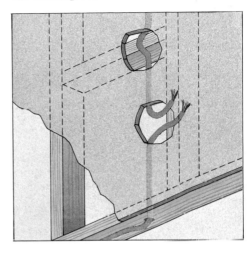

**C. Above:** Cables can usually be hidden in timber-framed walls, though you may have to use some ingenuity to cope with the framing members

## Timber-framed walls

With timber-framed walls, it is usually easy to drop cables down the hollow between the wall coverings on either side of the framing, fishing it out through a hole in the covering at the site of any switches or power points. At the top or bottom of the wall, you can either drill holes in the horizontal timber plates as you would with flooring joists. Or—especially where the wall is of lath and plaster—cut a small chase at these points and lead the cable round the plates. You will have to do something similar if you are unfortunate enough to encounter horizontal noggins along the site of the cable drop, or if you have to run the cable horizontally at any point (though in this case it is probably easier to replan so that horizontal runs are in the floor or across the ceiling).

# Install a 30 amp supply

Most homes in the UK are equipped with one or other of the two main types of 30 amp electrical circuit. Modern houses have a 30 amp ring circuit—a multi-outlet circuit supplying numerous 13 amp sockets and fixed appliances via fused outlets. Some older houses have a 30 amp multi-outlet radial circuit which supplies a limited number of 13 amp socket outlets and/or fixed appliances via fused outlets. In all cases, the outlets have a maximum capacity of 13 amps.

But some appliances, notably electric cookers and electric shower units, require their own separate 30 amp or 45 amp circuit (called a *radial final sub-circuit*) because of their high power rating.

Note that you should not confuse a 30 amp radial circuit with the older, 15 amp, 5 amp and 2 amp (round pin) radial circuits installed until about 1947. If you have one of these, your house is due for complete rewiring.

## Electric cooker circuit

Essentially, electric cooker circuits consist of a cable running from a circuit fuseway in the consumer unit to a control switch, and then on to the cooker itself.

The current rating of the fuse, or MCB (miniature circuit breaker), and of the cable in the circuit is determined by the current demand of the cooker. The majority of domestic electric cookers have a loading of between 10,000 watts and 13,000 watts. On the 240 volts electricity supply standard in the UK, the maximum possible current demand of a 10,000 watt cooker is 42 amps, and of a 13,000 watt cooker, 54 amps.

However, because of the oven thermostat and variable controls of the boiling rings, there will never be more than a momentary maximum demand. UK regulations provide a simple formula for

assessing the current demand of a domestic cooker, in which the first 10 amps are rated at 100 percent, and the remaining current at 30 percent. A socket connected to the control unit is rated at 5 amps.

This means that a socket and a 10,000 watt cooker drawing a theoretical 42 amps have an assessed demand of 25 amps. And a 13,000 watt cooker with a theoretical 54 amp demand, plus socket, is assessed as 28 amps. Consequently, most cookers fall well within a current rating of 30 amps. Only very large ones and those with double ovens require a 45 amp circuit.

## Consumer unit to control switch

Hopefully your existing consumer unit will have a spare fuseway from which to run the cable.

However, where there is no spare fuseway—and usually where you have a large cooker requiring a 45 amp circuit—you must install a separate mains switch and fuse unit, called a switchfuse unit.

## The cable

The only difference between a 45 amp and a 30 amp circuit is the size of the cable. If your calculations have shown you that a 30 amp fuse is adequate for your cooker, then you need cable with a current rating of at least 30 amps—6mm$^2$ twin and earth PVC sheathed will usually do. With a 45 amp fuse, 10mm$^2$ cable is needed.

The cable should obviously take the shortest possible route from the switchfuse unit to the cooker control unit. Where there are no solid floors it is an easy task to run the cable straight down from the switchfuse unit, under the floorboards, to emerge once again immediately below the planned position of the control unit.

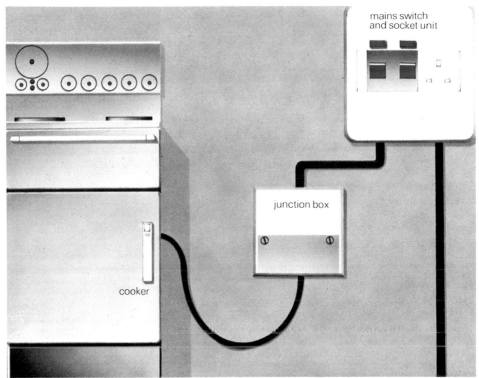

mains switch
and socket unit

junction box

cooker

**A. Above:** The 45 amp double-pole main switch and 13 amp switched socket is used in the circuit to the electric cooker to isolate the supply. The control unit is fixed at about 1.5m above floor level

However, should you need to run a cable across the direction of the joists, these must be drilled—not notched—at least 50mm below the top edge of the joist.

But, where, as in many kitchens, there is a solid floor, it is advisable to take the cable up from the switchfuse unit, into the ceiling void, across and between the joists, and then down the kitchen wall to the control switch.

### Positioning the control unit

The control unit is normally fixed at about 1.5m above floor level, and to one side of the cooker. UK regulations require that the switch should not be more than 2m from the cooker, to allow for rapid access in emergencies.

Control units come in various styles, either surface or flush mounting, with or without neon 'power' indicators, and with or without a kettle socket outlet. The current rating is usually 45 amps. If it is necessary to fix the switch above the cooker, one without a socket is recommended to avoid the risk of a flex trailing across a hot ring.

### Control unit to cooker

To allow a free-standing cooker to be moved for cleaning or servicing, you must run the last section of cable in the form of a trailing loop. The first few feet can either be fixed to or buried in the wall immediately below and behind the unit.

If you opt for burial, you must install an outlet box. You can either use a through box, simply anchoring the uncut cable with a clamp, or a terminal box, which would make it possible to remove the cooker altogether.

## Split-level cookers

In the UK, wiring regulations regard the separate hob and oven sections of a split-level cooker as a single unit. They should therefore be on one circuit—providing that both sections are sited within 2m of the control unit itself.

Following these rules, you can install the two sections up to 4m apart as long as the control unit is midway between them. And if one of the sections is installed more than 2m away from the control unit, it can share the circuit but needs a second control switch. In all cases, you must ensure that the cable fitted on the cooker side of the control unit is exactly the same size as the circuit cable.

## Electric shower unit circuit

An electric shower unit is an instantaneous electric water heater in which the water is heated as it flows over the element unit. To provide adequate hot water the element has a loading of 6000 watts or in some cases 7000 watts, with respective current demands of 26 and 29 amps.

To install a shower unit you will therefore need a 30 amp fuseway, a length of 6mm² twin and earth PVC sheathed cable, a double pole isolating switch, and a length of sheathed flexible cord or cable to connect the shower unit to the isolating switch. In some cases a flex, or *cord*, outlet unit is required for the final connection to the shower unit.

## Running the cable

On an electric shower installation, use a twin and earth PVC sheathed cable with

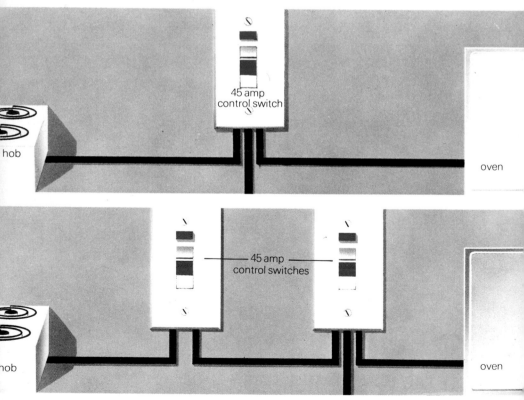

hob — 45 amp control switch — oven

hob — 45 amp control switches — oven

a current rating of not less than 30 amps to match the circuit fuse or MCB in the consumer unit. The circuit cable running from the 30 amp fuseway to the 30 amp double-pole isolating switch should run in the same way as that for a cooker.

It is dangerous to have an electric switch or socket within reach of wet hands, so you must install either a cord-operated ceiling switch in the bathroom or a wall-mounted switch outside (fig. C).

A special 30 amp double pole switch with neon indicator is available for cord operation and is mounted on a standard, square-moulded plastic box. To install this unit, first remove the knockout blank in the base for the two cables; one is the circuit cable, the other is the shower unit connecting cable. Pierce a hole in the ceiling for the two cables, connect them to the switch, then fix the unit to a timber joist using wood screws.

**B.** Use a 45 amp control switch without a socket if you prefer. If both sections of a split level are within 2m of the control unit, you can just use a single switch. **Above left**: A simple way of wiring a split level cooker circuit. **Below left**: Where the two sections are more than 4m apart it becomes necessary to use two cooker control units. **Right**: An alternative method of connecting up the oven and hob sections by linking them together in series—both the sections are controlled from the same switch in this method

Some shower units are supplied with a three-core circular sheathed flex. Do not remove this; instead, run both it and the cable from the isolating switch into a cord outlet unit mounted on a square-moulded plastic box and fixed near the shower unit.

In rooms other than the bathroom mount a 30 amp double-pole switch outside the showering cubicle, in a position where it cannot be reached by anyone using the shower.

## Connecting up the switch

The 30 amp cord-operated ceiling switch is a double-pole switch and therefore has two pairs of terminals. Each respective pair is marked L for live and N for neutral. One pair takes the cable from the consumer unit, and these are marked SUPPLY or MAINS. The other terminals are for the cable to the shower unit, and are marked LOAD.

## Connection at the consumer unit

With all the other wiring completed, your final task is to connect the cooker or shower circuit to the mains, either at a spare fuseway in the consumer unit or—if that is not possible—to a separate switchfuse unit.

To connect to a fuseway, turn off the mainswitch and remove the consumer unit cover. On some models you must first remove the fuse carriers or MCBs.

Cut the new circuit cable, allowing about 300mm for the inside of the unit.

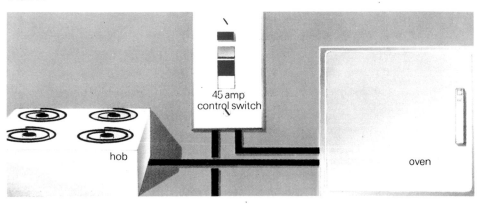

45 amp control switch

hob

oven

Trim about 250mm of outer sheathing from the cable, strip about 9mm of insulation from the live and neutral wires, then sheath all but 9mm of the bare earth wire with green and yellow PVC sleeving.

Next, knock out a blank from the consumer unit case and thread in the three wires until there is about 50mm of sheathing within the unit. Connect the red wire to the terminal of the spare fuseway, and the black wire to the neutral terminal block—which will already have some neutral wires connected to it in any case. Connect the sleeved earth wire to the common earth terminal block. Carefully replace the fuse carriers or MCBs, if you have had to remove these. Then put back the cover.

Finally, fit the new 30 amp fuse unit (or MCB), and if the fuse is rewirable, check that it contains a 30 amp fuse wire. Replace the cover of the consumer unit, turn on the mainswitch and you are ready to test the new installation. If any appliances refuse to work recheck the wiring very carefully.

## Connecting a fuse unit

Where there is no spare fuseway on an existing 30 amp consumer unit, or the circuit requires a 45 amp installation, you must install a switch-fuse unit.

In the UK, you cannot make the final connection to the meter yourself, but must contact the Electricity Board to do it for you. At the same time, they can check over the rest of your installation to ensure that it is safe.

A switchfuse unit is a one-way consumer unit consisting of a double-pole mainswitch and a single-pole fuseway fitted with either a fuse or an MCB (an MCB is best, and a cartridge fuse next

**C. Below:** In this type of shower installation, the double-pole cord operated switch is actually fitted to the bathroom ceiling. You should then run the supply cable through the ceiling and connect up the shower through a standard cord outlet unit

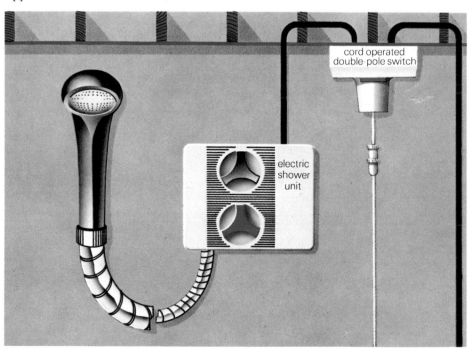

best). Both two-way and three-way consumer units are available, and you should consider installing these if future electrical extensions are anticipated.

Fit the unit to the wall adjacent to the existing consumer unit. Then connect three single-core, double insulated PVC sheathed cables—one with red, one with black, and one with green and yellow insulation—to the appropriate L (live), N (neutral) and earth mains terminals. The cables should be cut to about 1m in length, and then left for the Electricity Board to connect up. The Board stipulates the cable size—usually 16mm²—which is determined by the current rating of the Board's service fuse.

To prepare the end of the circuit cable

**D.** Sometimes it is necessary to install a switchfuse unit adjacent to the consumer unit from which to take the mains supply. Electricity Boards often insist that a 60 amp double-pole terminal block (below) is fitted adjacent to the meter—the Board has to connect it up by law

first cut it to the correct length, allowing a short amount for the inside of the switchfuse unit. Trim about 300mm of outer sheathing from the cable, strip about 9mm of insulation from the live and neutral wires, then sheath all but 9mm of the bare earth wire with green and yellow PVC sleeving.

Connect the wires to the appropriate fuseway terminals, insert the fuse unit if necessary then notify the Electricity Board that the circuit needs connecting to the mains.

### Earthing the fusebox

When the board makes the connections they may want to check the earthing of the installation. For safety's sake it's as well to check this yourself. The earth wire usually runs from the outside of the box to a nearby water pipe, gas pipe or some other metal object which runs to earth. Check the connections carefully, making sure that the earth wire is correctly bared and that the connections are tight and secure.

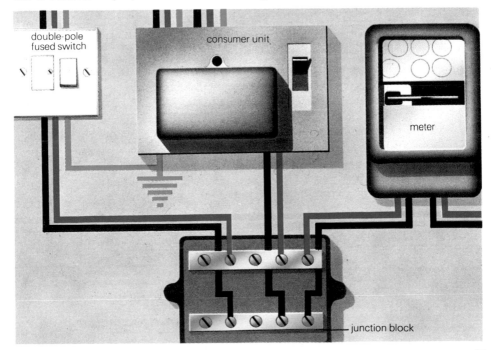

double-pole fused switch

consumer unit

meter

junction block

# Doorbell systems

Choosing a bell that is both efficient and yet attractive to look at is not an easy proposition. First you must decide whether you want to install a manual model or one powered by either batteries or mains electricity.

**Manual bells:** These are ideal if you do not want to be bothered with wiring or replacing batteries, but they are less sophisticated in appearance and often give a poor sound.

Manual bells are of two types. The most common—and strictly the only variety that is truly manual—consists of a metal bell, gong or plate which is struck once the doorbell is operated. Other manual bells have a wind-up clockwork mechanism and these usually give a ringing signal.

**Battery-operated bells:** These depend for their power on two or four small batteries stored inside the chime unit and save you having to check whether or not the mechanism is correctly wound.

**Electric bells:** Doorbells powered by mains electricity are by far the most popular since they have so many advantages over the more simple manual or battery-powered models. Unlike manual models (where the chime has to be mounted directly behind the push button) electric bell chimes can be fixed in almost any unobtrusive spot, providing they can be heard anywhere in the home. Indeed a single push button can operate more than one chime unit—providing this is wired correctly. Alternatively, you can connect more than one door push to a single unit, with two different signals so that you can tell whether someone is at a back or side door.

If you want something a little more unusual, you can install an electronic chime which plays one of a variety of tunes once the push button is depressed. These tunes can either be pre-selected by the householder or chosen at random by the unit.

## Transformers

All electric doorbells work on a very low voltage—usually between 3 and 12 volts—so you could not possibly connect them directly to the mains supply. Instead you must incorporate a transformer into the system, situated somewhere between the mains supply and the chime unit. Most manufacturers of doorbells will be able to supply you with a transformer suitable for this purpose.

## Door pushes

Once you have chosen which type of bell or chime unit you want to install you should turn your attention to the choice of button push. Care is needed here

**Below and right:** A whole range of different and unusual chime units is available so there is plenty of choice — both of the housings and signals

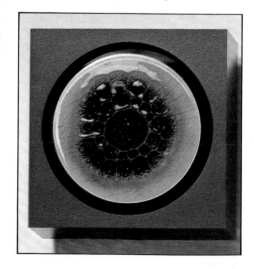

because the push must match the chime you have bought and also look attractive.

Door pushes come in a variety of sizes and widths, so choose one that fits neatly into place. They can be mounted either on the door itself or on the frame, but non-manual models are often better on the latter, because of the difficulties that might otherwise be caused by trailing wires as the door opens and closes.

## Fitting a manual or battery bell

Manual or battery-operated bell systems are easily fitted. All you need to do is to determine the position of the bell push, drill a hole in the door frame to accommodate it and then fit the push and chime unit into place.

Once you have finally decided on a suitable position for the bell, mark the spot carefully. To accommodate most manual or battery models you will need to drill a fairly large diameter hole all the way through the door or the adjoining frame. To avoid splitting the timber, fit a suitably sized twist or auger bit into a hand brace and drill through the wood slowly (fig. 1).

Try the bell for size before fitting it permanently in place.

The whole mechanism can then be screwed into position. Some models are held by screws driven through from the

front of the door while others are screwed from both sides. Once this is done, fit the chime unit into place—if necessary checking first that the batteries (if battery operated) are correctly seated. Finally, check that the bell is operating correctly. It should require little maintenance other than battery renewal, but it is a good idea to oil all the moving parts occasionally.

## Installing electric bells

Electric bells are not particularly difficult to install. The key to success lies in checking carefully where each component part goes and in tackling the work systematically.

Before you buy an electric bell decide first which type you want to install. You can then decide roughly where each of the component parts are to be mounted and from this calculate how much wire you will need to complete the job successfully. You should also decide at this stage whether you want to wire up just the front door or any back or side doors as well.

**Mounting the chime:** Once you have purchased your bell kit the first task is to position the chime unit. You should already have decided roughly where you want it—usually in the kitchen or the hall. But bear in mind that it should be heard both inside the house and also by the person pressing the button, otherwise the visitor will go on ringing the bell—something which might create mutual annoyance. Alternatively, you may want to fix up two chime units—perhaps one on each floor—so that if anyone comes to the door, the bell can be heard more easily.

In general the most suitable position for mounting chime units is about 2 m above ground level. At this height they produce the best sound and can usually be hidden away fairly unobtrusively. However, if you are installing an electronic chime, you may want to mount it slightly lower for easy adjustment.

**Mounting the push:** The techniques required to install an electric bell push are

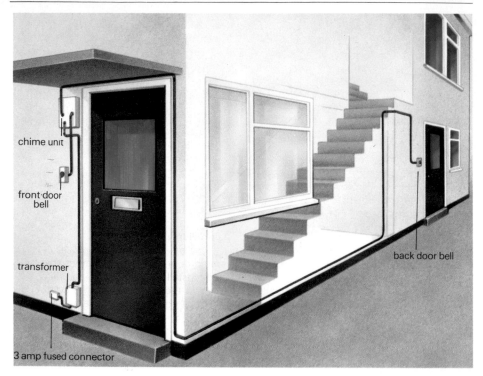

chime unit

front door bell

transformer

3 amp fused connector

back door bell

the same as those used to fix a manual model except that the hole you need to drill to accommodate the push is generally smaller.

Once the push and the chime are in position you can wire one to another. The push should be connected to the output terminals on the chime and the wire fixed neatly around the room with cable clips.

**Wiring the chime unit:** If your chime unit is not powered by batteries it needs to be connected to the mains electric supply via a transformer.

First, fix the transformer securely to the wall. It can be mounted next to the chime or in some other less obtrusive position between the chime and the power source. Once it has been secured firmly in position, wire the output terminals of the transformer to the relevant terminals on the chime according to the maker's instructions.

The next stage is to connect the input

**A. Above:** An electric bell system employing a two-tone chime, which is then connected up to both the front and the back doorbell pushes

side of the transformer. One solution would be to plug the transformer into a nearby socket outlet, using a length of mains flex (not bell wire). But this could tie up a valuable outlet.

A better solution is to treat the transformer as a fixed appliance and connect it permanently into the house wiring.

In the UK, the transformer could be wired into a ring main via a fused connection unit fitted with a 3 amp fuse.

Alternatively, because of the low current needed to operate a chime, it is also possible to connect it into a lighting circuit. And as the transformer is likely to be mounted near the ceiling this may be easier and neater than trying to connect it to a power circuit. Connect the transformer to a suitable outlet as if it

**1** To fit a bell push, start by drilling a hole through the door frame using either a hand-held brace or alternatively an electric drill with a large diameter bit. Then carefully thread the wire through from the back. Try to ensure that the cable has no kinks in it and that the plastic sheathing remains intact

**2** An illuminated bell push can only be fitted as a part of an electrically operated doorbell system. Before you actually install it you need to carefully check that the small bulb in the system is correctly in position and undamaged before you proceed with any more of the installation work

**3** Bare the ends of both wires and attach one to each of the two retaining screws, which are located just inside the bell push housing. Then you should turn the bell push system over and screw it firmly and securely to the door frame. If the push has a see-through section for a name card to be fitted to it, this can then be inserted

**4** Lead the wire back inside the hall, pinning it neatly, every so often, to the top of the skirting board or running it in conduit, until you reach the chime unit. If you are also installing a back doorbell push, fix this in position at this stage and then run the wires to the chime unit, keeping them out of sight as much as it is possible

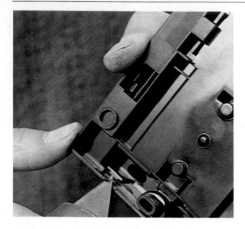

**5** Before you fix up the chime unit, use a sharp handyman's knife to clear each of the wire entry points, which are located on the back of the unit. Then secure the unit firmly to the wall using the necessary wall plugs. To ensure that the sound carries it should be positioned about 2m above ground level

**6** Having secured the chime unit in place, the next task is to fix the transformer firmly into position. This can be located in a suitable spot anywhere between the chime unit and the spur connection to the electricity mains. Then you should connect up the back of a 3 amp fused unit to the wall

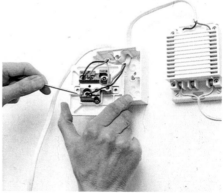

**7** Connect the wires from both the front and back doorbell pushes to the output side of the chime unit according to all the manufacturer's instructions. Then link up the input side of the chime unit with the transformer, taking care to choose the two terminals that give the correct voltage needed for this particular type of bell unit

**8** The wiring is completed by connecting the transformer input to the fused connection unit and then linking this to the mains. You can then replace the fronts of each box and check that all the wiring is pinned neatly to the wall out of sight. Finally check that you have the right fuse in the connection unit, turn on the power and test the system

were an extra light—though of course you will not need to provide it with a switch as you want the connection to be permanently live.

## Complex wiring schemes

Most people will probably be content to have a single bell push mounted on the front door. But if visitors often call at more than one entrance you can easily fit up a second bell push on a side or back door, wired to a central unit.

If you want to do this you should buy a chime unit which has a dual tone. This gives a different sound from each of the different pushes—even though both pushes are wired to the same chime. In this way you can tell whether someone is at the front door or the back door.

**B. Below**: Doorbell systems incorporating telephones are easily installed and give a greater degree of security than the traditional bell unit

The only problem you may have is in connecting the wires to the transformer. Most transformers are capable of being wired to more than one bell push, but you should seek advice from the manufacturer before you attempt to do this.

## Door security devices

Increasingly a number of sophisticated devices are being used to complement or even take the place of traditional doorbells. The most popular of these—available in kit form for the do-it-yourselfer—consists of a speaker system linked from the front door to a telephone situated inside the house. The system gives the householder a greater degree of security than the traditional push bell and its very presence can often deter burglars and house thiefs.

The door security system is connected up in a very similar way to the electric bell system (see above) with a small speaker unit in place of the push button.

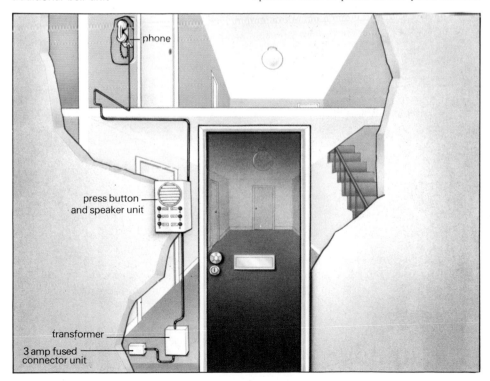

phone

press button and speaker unit

transformer

3 amp fused connector unit

# Installing a burglar alarm

Burglary is one of the most worrying types of crime to both householders and flat dwellers alike. Not only are possessions vulnerable: senseless vandalism and personal attack have become increasingly common.

Burglar alarms help to make your home secure in a number of ways: they warn you of an intruder if you are asleep at night; they alert your neighbours if a burglar strikes while you are away; their presence helps deter would-be thieves; and the sound of the alarm should frighten a burglar out of your home

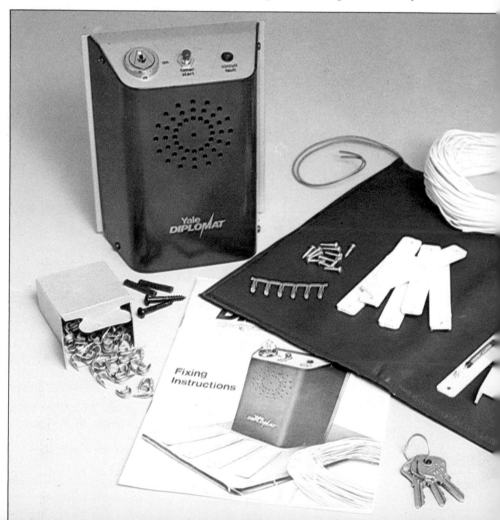

before he has a chance to take anything or do any damage to your property.

## Types of burglar alarm

There are several types of alarm available, some of which you can fit yourself. *Ultrasonic detectors* are alarms that employ frequency sound pulses generated by a tiny speaker. The pulses are bounced off room surfaces and are constantly monitored by a microphone, usually housed in the same unit. Any change in the sound pattern triggers the alarm.

The disadvantages of this system are that they may be triggered by such things as traffic noise or blustery wind, and they

cannot really be used while you are still moving around elsewhere in the house.

*Microwave detectors* work on a similar principle to ultrasonic detectors, except that they use radio waves. This kind of alarm is simple to fit, is easily disguised, and very effective. It is less prone to false alarms than the ultrasonic system, but, again, is of little use when the house is occupied.

The basis of electronic loop systems is an unbroken wiring circuit, along which is strung a number of different sensors, all fixed at strategic points. There is nothing to stop you moving about the house once the system is activated.

*Open* circuits are completed when one of the sensors is activated. As soon as current flows, the control box triggers a bell or siren. The bell circuit is electrically latched so that it cannot be switched off except by a master key.

*Closed* circuit systems are kept alert by a trickle of electric current. When a sensor is activated the circuit is broken and this triggers the alarm in the same way as an open circuit.

Alarm systems of this type are available for do-it-yourself fittings. Electronic loop systems can be powered by mains or battery, or a combination of the two to guard against mains failure.

A projected beam of invisible light aligned between an emitter and a sensor forms the system used by *infra-red detectors*. If the infra-red beam is broken, the alarm is triggered. To increase their effectiveness, beams can be laced over an area using a series of reflectors. Such systems are complex to install, and are best left to a professional security firm.

## Types of sensor

Sensors are the detection devices fitted along a loop circuit to doors and windows and other possible break-in

**Left:** Several different types of burglar alarm kits are available for the do-it-yourselfer. They can be mains or battery operated but a combination of both is the ideal system

entry points. When a door is opened or a window smashed the circuit is disrupted and the alarm is activated.

There are several types of sensor on the market:

A *microswitch sensor* is a tiny electrical switch activated by a plunger arrangement. The plunger is held down by a closed door or window to complete a closed circuit. If that door or window is opened, the plunger is released, breaking the circuit and triggering the alarm.

A *magnetic reed contact* is a very simple sensor which is featured in very many alarm packages in one form or another. Current is passed through two fine magnetic reeds, sealed in a glass tube. The tube is fitted in a case, in line with the loop circuit, to the frame of a door (or certain types of windows). A

**A.** Microwave and ultrasonic detectors should be positioned to scan entry points

similar case containing a magnet is fitted adjacent to the reed tube, on or in the door itself. The two cases are fitted parallel to each other at the opening edge of the door, usually less than 3–5mm apart. It is particularly important that the two halves of this sensor are correctly aligned.

While the door remains closed, the magnet holds the two concealed reeds together to complete a closed circuit. If the door is then opened by more than the release distance the reeds spring apart and activate the alarm. Concealment is important, as an experienced burglar will certainly be able to use a magnet to keep the reeds together as the door is opened.

*Metallic foil detectors* are available in self-adhesive rolls for attachment to window glass. Current flows down the foil in a closed circuit and if the window is broken, this is disrupted and the alarm sounds.

Metallic foil detectors have the advantage of advertising to the would-be intruder that your home is protected. They should be fitted to the inside of the glass, close to any window catches.

*Vibration contacts* are taking over from metallic foil as window sensors because they look neater, are easier to install, and are a better safeguard for modern, large-area widows. They are closed circuit devices contained in self-adhesive cases which can be mounted at suitable points on the glass itself. Heavy vibration breaks the circuit and the alarm sounds.

Most installations also include one or more *pressure mats*. These are open-circuit devices, wired up to a separate pair of contacts in the control box (fig. 7). An intruder stepping on the mat completes the circuit and activates the alarm.

Pressure mats must be installed against a firm floor, under both carpet and underfelt.

*Panic buttons* (or personal attack buttons) are open circuit devices linked to their own separate terminals in the control box and, usually, they can be kept constantly activated during the day. If you are attacked by an intruder, you

alarm bell (wires concealed) located conspicuously but out of reach

panic button near bed

**B.** It is sometimes advisable to fit an exterior alarm at the back of the house where it is least noticeable. Panic buttons can be sited by your bed.

press the button to activate the alarm.

## Loop alarm kits

Most alarm kits come complete with a range of different sensors; they also contain wiring and instructions for linking them to the *control box*. This contains a number of terminals for connection of open circuits, closed circuits, panic buttons and—some-times—smoke detectors.

Into the control box comes electric power to maintain the closed circuits in the alert mode and to power the alarm bell itself.

Some systems rely entirely on battery power. They use very small currents to maintain the circuits, but the batteries drain rapidly once the alarm is sounded.

The disadvantage of a mains-powered system is that it is affected by power cuts. Also, the power and alarm bell cables must both be well concealed to prevent

tampering, as the easiest way to im-mobilize this kind of an alarm system is to disconnect either of these.

The best alarm kits use a combination of mains and battery power so that if the mains fails or is tampered with, the system switches automatically to battery power.

All alarm systems have some kind of keyed *master control switch* which enables you to set the alarm and turn it off. There is usually a time delay to give you a few seconds to enter or leave the house or get away from the alarm-sensitive areas.

Some systems merely have a key switch on the control box. Others can incorporate remote switches and these may be elsewhere in the house, often by the front door.

Alarm systems usually make use of small bells that produce a very loud sound. Once the bell is activated it can only be turned off by the master switch key.

The purpose of interior bells is to frighten the intruder out of your house, so locate these in an inaccessible spot such as at the top of the stair well. Exterior bells, which come in weather-proof cases, are intended to alert neigh-bours and passers-by. They should be in-stalled high, out of reach, with the wiring to them passing directly through the wall to prevent tampering.

## Planning and fitting the system

When you plan your alarm system, concentrate the alarm sensors at vulner-able points such as windows and doors, and around any inside region where the burglar is likely to go—such as the hallway. Start by thoroughly surveying your ground floor and draw up a plan, noting the vulnerable areas likely. Mark out a circuit line for the closed circuit sensors which links them up in the most economical way.

All doors to the outside should be in-cluded in the closed loop, especially those with any areas of glass such as slid-ing patio doors. The latter can be fitted

57

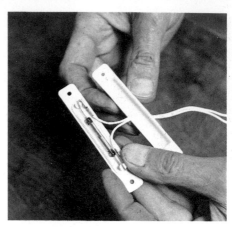

**1** Plan a convenient location for the alarm control box and mark the position of fixing holes for this. Then screw the box firmly into place

**2** If necessary, wire up the magnetic reed contacts using wire provided with the kit. Check that the magnetic action is in satisfactory working order

**5** For a cylindrical reed sensor, drill a hole in the frame. Then wire up the reed contact and put it carefully in the hole. Feed the wire into the back

**6** Fit the magnet section neatly into a hole drilled in the door edge. Then connect up the reed contact to the closed circuit loop

with a magnetic reed sensor that is shielded from the metal.

Fit sensors to some interior doors as well.

All ground-floor windows are vulnerable, but pay special attention to large bay windows, and windows concealed

from general view at the back of the house and down alleyways. Fit either metallic tape sensors or vibration sensors.

Fit pressure mats at strategic points, such as at the bottom of the stairs or in front of valuable objects. Small pressure

**3** The reed section of the sensor is located on the door frame. In some types of kit, this is set into the woodwork to remain completely out of view

**4** Shut the door and butt the magnet section against the reed section and screw into place. Then pin the wires to the corner and behind the door frame

**7** Another commonly used sensor is a pressure mat, which is best located near a likely entry point or passageway or close to valuables

**8** All connecting wires should be completely concealed from view to discourage tampering—but this is not an essential requirement for closed circuits

mats can be fitted up the stairs.

Locate the control box in a position that is out of sight, but not so far from the door that you cannot leave the house having just activated the system. The control box is fixed to the wall, or a mounting panel, using plugs and screws.

Where wiring must cross a door, run it under the carpet, over the door frame or through a flexible door cable, which most kits offer as an accessory. Power and alarm bell connections should be concealed at ground level: if possible run the wiring beneath floorboarding.

# Installing fluorescent lighting

Fluorescent lights with their characteristic, glare-free light are today very much a part of the home lighting scene. And placed with care, they can create effects well beyond the capabilities of ordinary light bulbs.

Their light output, measured in lumens per watt, varies according to the colour of the light, but for general lighting it is more than three times that of an incandescent bulb. For example, the light output of a 40 watt fluorescent tube is about the same as that of two 100 watt bulbs.

The main disadvantage of fluorescent lighting is that it produces a shadowless light which can destroy the attractive character of a room. Although the hard shadows produced by some tungsten lights can be objectionable and dangerous in the vicinity of stairways, a living room without shadows can be unbearable.

## Choice of colour

Fluorescent tubes are available in either 'warm' or 'cool' colours, and whereas the cool colours—such as the 'natural' commonly found in offices—may be acceptable in the domestic garage or workshop, you are likely to need a much warmer colour in a living area.

For example, the Philips Softone 32, or a de-luxe warm white tube has good colour rendering and a warm colour similar to that of tungsten lighting. These features make it and similar lamps particularly suitable for decorative lighting above curtains, pictures and cupboards.

Circular lamps are found only in the warm white series, but because they are normally enclosed by a decorative diffuser of either plain or tinted glass, lamp colour itself is not critical.

## Types of tube

The standard straight fluorescent tubes are made in a number of lengths and wattages, ranging from 125 watt down to 15 watt and 2400mm down to 450mm, though 40 watt tubes, either 1200mm or 600mm long, are common.

Miniature tubes are also available. These are from about 525mm long down to as little as 150mm and are rated at only a few watts. They are typically used in shaving mirrors, cooker hoods and inspection lamps.

Circular fluorescent tubes are made in a number of sizes—from 60 and 40 watt, both 400mm diameter, down to tubes of about half that size.

## Installing a fluorescent fitting

The typical domestic fluorescent fitting consists of a metal batten or casing, which contains the ballast gear, switch-starter (where appropriate) and associated components including a capacitor, internal wiring and a terminal block. Two bi-pin lampholders project from the underside of the batten to support the tube.

Note: Remember never to work on a circuit until you are certain power is switched off at the mains and it is not live.

Start by removing the cover of the batten to gain access to the cable entry holes, the screw fixing holes and the terminal block. Decide where you want to position the fitting, then hold it against the fixing surface and use a bradawl to

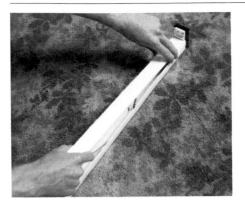

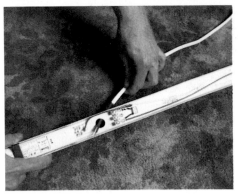

**1** To wire up a standard fluorescent light, start by removing the diffuser (if there is one) then unclip the cover from the body of the fitting

**2** Feed in the appropriate length of 1.5mm$^2$ twin and earth PVC cable through the large hole that is punched in the back of the fitting

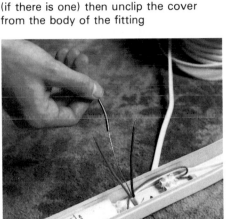

**3** Before you go any further, make sure that the bare earth wire is covered with a suitable length of green and yellow PVC sleeving insulation

**4** Next connect up the wires in the cable to their appropriate terminals inside the fitting—red to L, black to N, and green and yellow to Earth

mark the screw holes. Bear in mind that where you are replacing an existing fitting you may have to allow for the position of the cables already there.

In the case of a ceiling mounting, once you have marked the holes check where they fall in relation to the joists. If one or more holes are between joists, you may have to drill additional holes in the base of the fitting or fit a piece of timber

between the joists in the relevant place. But in many cases, slightly adjusting the fitting position saves either task.

Before handling the existing wiring, remember to turn off the electricity and to remove the appropriate fuse or fuses. Once you have arranged the cable run to the fitting (see below), feed this through the entry hole then secure the fitting to the ceiling using No. 8 woodscrews.

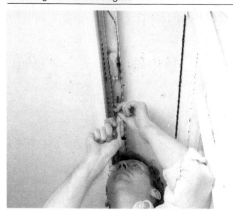

**5** Use the fitting as a template for marking the fixing positions. Check that these are really secure before you finally screw the fitting in place

**6** If you cannot actually get to the ceiling void, run the cable down a door or window frame and then take the supply from a fused spur

**7** Make sure that the connections in the fitting have not dislodged themselves during installation, then you can put the cover back in position

**8** Finally, fit the tube itself. Check that it is securely held in the bi-pin lampholders at either end before you attempt to switch on

### Wiring up

If you are replacing an existing light fitting, it is possible in most cases to use the cable from this for the new installation. Having prepared the ends of the cable as necessary, simply connect the wires to the terminal block on the fitting.

The one exception is where your fluorescent light is of the *switchless* type

and your lighting circuit of the older, non-earthed variety. In this case you must run a length of $1.5mm^2$ single-core PVC insulated non-sheathed cable from the earth terminal in the consumer unit to that of the fitting.

Where the new fitting is to replace two or more lights on the same circuits, the wires to these must be disconnected and drawn back to a junction box situated

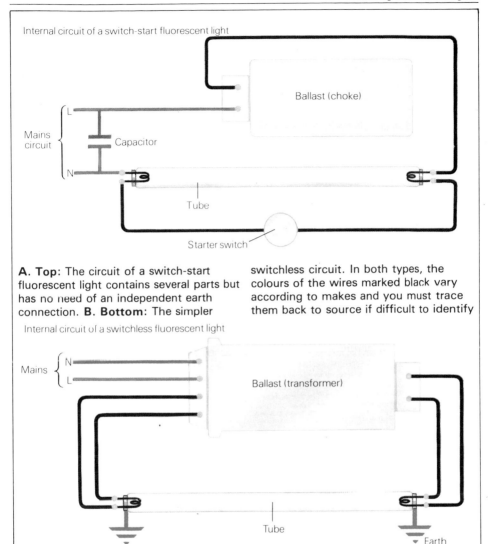

Internal circuit of a switch-start fluorescent light

Ballast (choke)

L

Mains circuit

Capacitor

N

Tube

Starter switch

**A. Top**: The circuit of a switch-start fluorescent light contains several parts but has no need of an independent earth connection. **B. Bottom**: The simpler

switchless circuit. In both types, the colours of the wires marked black vary according to makes and you must trace them back to source if difficult to identify

Internal circuit of a switchless fluorescent light

Mains

N

L

Ballast (transformer)

Tube

Earth

in the ceiling void.

Entirely new installations can be wired either from the lighting circuit or from a 5 amp fused spur taken off the ring main. Where access to the ceiling void is easy, the former is usually the obvious choice. Identify and break into the three-way junction box and light switch, then run a new length of cable to the fitting.

But where the new installation is to be

at a lower level—such as underneath fitted cupboards above a worksurface—it is often easier to take a switched fused spur from the ring main, fit this adjacent to the installation and then connect it to the batten or holder.

## Other fittings

Circular fluorescent fittings are even simpler to fix than the strip type. Simply secure the metal backplate to the fixing surface and connect the wires to the cable connector, then install the lamp and fit the diffuser.

Shaving lights, bulkhead fittings and other miniature tube lighting fittings are fixed and connected in the same way as ordinary light fittings.

For pelmet lighting use the thin, batten type of fitting with reflector tubes to produce maximum downward light. Though the fittings are installed in the normal way, positioning is important if the right effect is to be achieved. The lights must be no less than 150mm in front of the curtains, two or more tubes must be overlapped to prevent dark patches, and the end of the tube (or tubes) must extend a good 50mm beyond the curtain width.

## Dimmer switching

It is not possible to use an ordinary dimmer switch to control a fluorescent light. Where a fluorescent fitting replaces a tungsten filament light controlled by a dimmer switch, it is simpler to replace the dimmer with an ordinary type of switch.

## How fluorescent lights work

The most important component in a fluorescent light is the glass tube. This is coated on the inside with a fluorescent powder, and contains mercury vapour and a small amount of argon gas to assist starting. At each end of the tube is an electrode with a small heating element—similar to the filament of an ordinary light bulb—which is coated with an electron-emitting substance.

When an electric current is applied to the heated electrodes, electrons flow along the inside of the tube. These bombard the glass, causing the powder to fluoresce and so produce the characteristic light.

Once it has been started, a fluorescent tube needs nowhere near as much current as an ordinary bulb. Consequently, it requires a controlling device called a *ballast* to limit the flow of current. The ballast and its associated components are usually contained in the fluorescent fitting.

There are two methods of starting, or 'striking', the flow of electrons in the tube. The first, termed the *switch-start*, uses a starter switch—a canister similar in appearance to the flasher unit of a motor car or 35mm film canister—which is installed in the side of the fitting. The other is known as the *switchless* or 'quick start' because there is no delay between switching on the light and the tube striking in the familiar 'flashing manner'.

When a switch-start fluorescent light is switched on, current flows through the ballast unit—which contains a choke—on to the starter and then through the electrode heaters. After a short interval, the switch starter contacts open and produce a surge of high voltage from the choke which is discharged between the heated electrodes to start the continuous flow of electrons and keep the tube alight. The job of the switch is then finished, though the choke remains in circuit to control the current flow.

When a switchless fluorescent light is switched on, current flows through a transformer, which has a low voltage tapping to the electrodes, causing them to emit electrons. The high voltage surge which starts the flow of electrons is provided by a special earthed tube, which has a metal strip running from one end to the other and is earthed to the circuit through the lamp caps.

When installing a switchless fluorescent fitting or replacing a tube, you must therefore make sure that the tube is of the switchless type; although a switchless tube will operate in a switch-start fitting, the opposite does not apply.

A fluorescent tube has an average life of 7000 hours compared with 1000 hours for a standard electric light bulb. For average use this represents over ten years of life.

When a fluorescent tube fails it does not fail completely like a tungsten bulb. Instead it behaves in a characteristic manner usually flashing on and off or dimming before the light finally fails.

# Concealed lighting

Use fluorescent lights to give an effective treatment to high, narrow or badly lit corridors.

Many older houses with high ceilings have corridors that are very tall and narrow and difficult to light. Fitting a suspended ceiling reduces the height and alters the proportion of the corridor.

This design includes circular fluorescent lights for a spread of even, bright light. They are concealed behind a pierced grid, which gives an interesting surface and patterns the light. It is based on commercially available, pre-formed chipboard ceiling panels, but you can use softwood slats as an alternative. The pre-formed panels are 600mm square, so you will have to fit your design to this size and add intermediate supports for ceilings with a larger span.

Fit bearer battens to the wall and add a soffit on which to support the lights. The latter are simple 300mm diameter tubes with a remote choke. Paint the soffit matt black then clip the tubes in place and wire them up.

The ceiling panels are held to the battens by sliding clip fittings designed for the purpose.

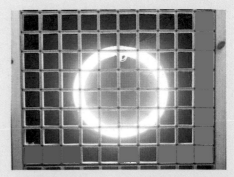

# Spot and track lighting

The traditional method of lighting a room—a single central bulb hanging from the ceiling—leaves a lot to be desired. True, the light levels in the room may be enough for most purposes, but a single bulb makes for a very stark lighting scheme with little atmosphere.

There are many ways of creating this elusive atmosphere using carefully planned lighting systems, but one of the most effective is to use spotlights.

Spotlights—whether mounted like an ordinary ceiling or wall light, or on lengths of track—can be used for two main purposes: task lighting, where they serve to illuminate a desk or working surface; and mood lighting, where they play on and subtly highlight pictures, ornaments and plants.

## Choosing spotlights

Once you have decided how a room is to be used and decorated you must decide how to light it. At first glance the choice of available light fittings is bewildering, but your first priority is to choose the type of spotlight bulb (more correctly called the lamp) that will give you the type of illumination you want.

There are four basic types of spotlight lamp in general use: the general lamp service (GLS); the internally silvered lamp (ISL); the crown-silvered lamp (CS); and the parabolic aluminized reflector (PAR) lamp. They all give roughly the same amount of light for a given wattage, but because they concentrate and diffuse the light in different ways, each produces a different intensity of light at any particular distance.

**GLS lamps:** This is an ordinary light bulb and must therefore be mounted in a reflective light fitting. The beam of light emitted is broad and diffused, but up to 2m away from the subject a 60 watt lamp

**Left:** Spotlights and track lighting look far more complicated to install than they actually are. For a modest outlay and a little work you can greatly alter (and often improve) the lighting and atmosphere in any of the rooms in your home

is sufficient for reading.

**ISL lamps:** Probably the most common spotlamp of all, the back of the lamp is silvered so that nearly all the light output is in a strongly directional beam with a 35° spread. Used in the same way as the GLS lamp and at the same wattage the ISL gives a higher level of illumination.

**CS lamps:** These are silvered at the front so that the light is reflected back to a parabolic reflector in the fitting. The resulting forward-facing beam has a concentrated spread of about 15°, which gives a very intense level of light around the subject. This beam is seen to best effect when mounted on a high (4m) ceiling and used to illuminate a table.

**PAR lamps:** These have a parabolic reflector and are available with coloured lenses. They can be bought as spotlights with a narrow beam or floodlights with a wide beam and because they are totally sealed they can be used out of doors.

**Lamp caps:** All four types of lamp are available with one of three caps (the part that goes into the fitting) namely, bayonet, single centre contact, and Edison screw. Like ordinary lamps, the smaller sizes have smaller caps.

## Types of light fitting

Once you have decided which type of lamp is best suited to each lighting position, you can choose a light fitting that will take it.

CS lamps, for example, need a parabolic reflector—and this obviously restricts your choice of fittings somewhat. GLS lamps also need a reflector of some sort, though unless you need a fairly concentrated beam of light the shape of the reflector is not so important. With ISL and PAR lamps no reflector is necessary to control the spread and shape of the light beam, so the choice of fitting open to you is potentially vast.

**Controlling glare:** Glare can be an irritating problem when reading or working. CS lamps with their narrow beams do not create much sideways glare, but others almost certainly will. The answer in this case is to use a recessed fitting.

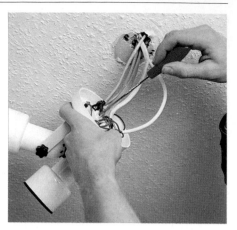

**1** When you decide you want to install a recessed spotlight, start by selecting a suitable site for it, then use a cardboard template and pencil to mark its position clearly on the selected ceiling. Then drill a hole carefully through the ceiling inside the circle and cut carefully around the circumference of the marked-out hole with a padsaw

**2** When you have cut out the hole in the ceiling and taken care not to damage any of the surrounding plaster work, you can draw a power supply from a nearby loop-in ceiling rose. This can be very easily done by connecting heat-resistant cable to the existing ceiling rose and then running it along to the position of the new lamp

**5** An important point which should always be carefully noted when you decide to fit a recessed spotlight into the ceiling is to make sure you get the correct match of lamp and fitting. The particular fitting detailed does not feature a reflector unit, so the only lamps that will be really suitable for it are the ISL or PAR type of lighting units

**6** If you decide you want to power a section of track light from a loop-in ceiling rose, replace the two-core flex running to the lampholder with a length of three-core flex. Next you should strip off the sheathing and insulation from the flex and connect it up to the track's electrical adaptor—this is also known as the 'live end'

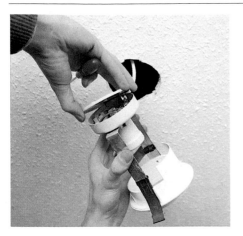

3 Connect up the heat-resistant cable to the recessed fitting at its other end. In this particular case no thermal insulation was necessary to protect the roof space area. You can then fit the protective cover safely over the terminals, but make sure that the cable sheathing does not finish short of this box so as to expose the cores

4 This unit has adjustable steel brackets that rest on the ceiling and support its weight. Set them correctly and then slip the fitting into the hole. To prevent any disturbance from glare many recessed spotlights have a black ribbed drum on the inside. Slip this in place inside the fitting before you actually install the selected lamp

7 Screw the light track to the ceiling using woodscrews and cavity plugs, plug in the electrical adaptor, and then snap the conducting strip firmly into place. The next stage is to clip the top cover into position on the electrical adaptor, making sure the flex insulation terminates well inside the actual unit and that it does not overlap

8 You can buy an adaptor which replaces the ceiling rose of a joint box system. The unit is screwed to the ceiling and the live end is wired up in the normal way. Fix the track to the ceiling next to the adaptor, plug in the live end adaptor, and then screw the top cover in place to neatly conceal the hole and all the flex

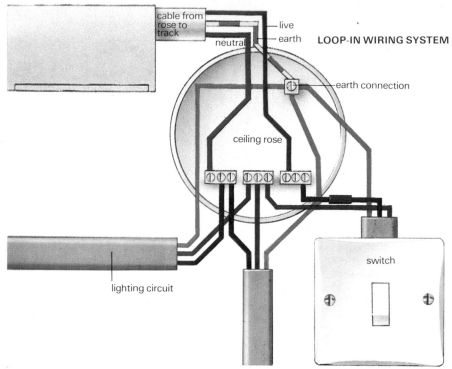

cable from rose to track

live

earth

neutral

**LOOP-IN WIRING SYSTEM**

earth connection

ceiling rose

switch

lighting circuit

## Types of mounting

Light fittings are often mounted on adjustable brackets so that the light beam can be pointed in any direction. Many fittings can be mounted directly on walls or ceilings, and most can also be bought with special adaptors for mounting on tracks.

Light fittings are available for recessing into a ceiling. Most are fixed so that the bulb points straight down—a *downlighter* —and drum-type fittings are the most popular. Other fittings have baffles which push the light out more horizontally than vertically. These are known as *wallwashers* because they are often used to illuminate a picture below them or part of the wall.

## Track lighting

One disadvantage of having permanently mounted spotlights is that you cannot alter the character of the lighting system in a room without a great deal of trouble.

For this reason, track lighting with its built-in flexibility has become extremely popular. A light track is a length of metal or plastic incorporating continuous live, neutral and earth conductors which cannot be touched accidentally. This is screwed to the wall or ceiling and spotlights are then mounted on it using special adaptors. The lights can be slid along the track, mounted or dismounted easily, and all the lights on one track operate from the same power supply.

Track generally comes in lengths of about 1m; some makes can be cut shorter, while all makes clip together to form longer lengths or different shapes. The electricity supply is connected to an adaptor which clips into one end. Some light fitting adaptors have built-in switches so that you can switch lights on and off individually, but unless you use adaptors with pull-cord switches this may present problems.

The most important thing to remember

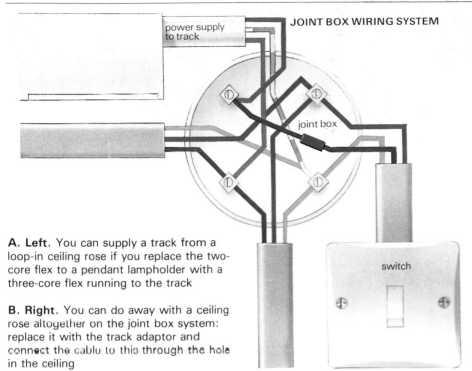

JOINT BOX WIRING SYSTEM

power supply to track

joint box

switch

**A. Left.** You can supply a track from a loop-in ceiling rose if you replace the two-core flex to a pendant lampholder with a three-core flex running to the track

**B. Right.** You can do away with a ceiling rose altogether on the joint box system: replace it with the track adaptor and connect the cable to this through the hole in the ceiling

about track is that it is not always possible to mix and match it with light fittings and adaptors; if you are considering buying a track lighting system, make sure you can get light fittings.

## Installation

The installation details that follow refer mainly to UK wiring practice. Wherever you live, never take chances with electricity: *switch off* at the mains and check the current is dead before starting work.

Spotlight fittings are installed in much the same way as other light fittings, but there are two special factors to take into account.

First, there is a limit to the number of lights you can have on a circuit. In the UK, most lighting circuits are 5 amp, and the practical limit is 12 lamps—which can soon be reached if you plan to add several spotlights to an existing circuit. There are two main ways round this

problem. You can install an extra lighting circuit—if you have a spare fuseway on the consumer unit (fuseboard)—or you can fit an additional consumer unit. Or you can connect some lights to a ring main circuit. You can take a spur off the ring main at any convenient point, and wire it using 2.5mm$^2$ cable to a fused connection unit fitted with a 13 amp fuse. From this, you can run a circuit using 1.5mm$^2$ cable for up to 24 lamps, incorporating switches and so on as for any lighting circuit.

Of course, if you have room on an existing circuit, you can wire spotlights in a number of ways. If you are replacing an existing fitting, or adding a light to be run off the same switch, simply wire to the existing ceiling rose. For a separate light with its own switch, you can either run the new circuit from a loop-in rose if there is one conveniently placed or from a new joint box fitted into the existing lighting circuit. Many fittings have only

**Above**: Several kinds of spotlights can be used to create bright or subdued effects

three wiring terminals inside: if you want to wire such a fitting on the loop-in system, you will have to add an additional terminal block to the fitting for the switch wire.

The second problem is that old lighting circuits have no earth wire. For spotlights that need earthing, you will have to run an earth wire from the fitting back to the consumer unit.

Many fittings have no backing plate on the mounting piece: the UK wiring regulations require such a plate. One solution is to fix the mounting piece over a circular conduit junction box.

### Installing track lighting

In general, track lighting installation is the same as for other fittings: the track is screwed to the wall or ceiling and the lights are then plugged into it.

You can draw the power supply for the track in many of the ways described above. But the electrical adaptor pieces are usually rather small and do not allow room for you to add a loop-in terminal, so you may need to use the joint-box method of wiring.

### Recessed fittings

Most manufacturers offer light fittings that can be recessed into the ceiling to be used as downlighters and wall-washers. There are two basic types: one is dropped through a hole in the ceiling from above

and is supported by brackets which rest on the ceiling; the other is offered up from below and has a bezel which is screwed to the ceiling using woodscrews and plugs.

Before buying and fitting recessed light fittings there are a few points to consider: first of all make sure that there is sufficient space above ceiling level for the fitting; secondly check that there are no restrictions on how close to a ceiling joist you can mount the fitting; and thirdly ensure that there is no way that the fitting could overheat and become potentially dangerous.

The last point is very important, as spotlights operate at very high temperatures. Follow any fitting instructions closely, if necessary lining the nearest joists and laths and the undersides of the floorboards above with asbestos mat to protect them from the heat. If you are mounting the fittings into a ceiling with a loft or roof space above it, keep any thermal insulation well away from the fitting or it will overheat very quickly. The best solution is to make a heat-resistant housing for the fitting, over which you can re-lay the insulation.

You may be required to use heat-resistant flex within 1m of the fitting. In this case, run the flex from the fitting and connect it to the power cable and the switch using a suitable joint-box wiring system.

# Free-standing lamps

The passing of the oil lamp should be mourned. It represented a highly civilized form of domestic lighting for two obvious reasons—it could be easily moved to where light was needed and you could adjust brightness. An additional bonus was the colour temperature of the oil light, which was 'warm', because it was primarily at the red end of the colour spectrum.

Contrast this to the stark and clinical cold/blue light produced by a ceiling-mounted fluorescent tube, and you can soon appreciate the advantages of localized, warm lighting.

Table or standard lamps have super-seded oil lamps and these generally use hot filaments, which also give off light towards the red end of the spectrum. They are movable, as far as the lamp flex will allow, and, by selecting a suitable wattage bulb, can be adjusted for brightness.

In addition to being used to provide localized light—for reading, needlework or even background illumination for TV viewing—standard and table lamps can also, if carefully located, be used to give dramatic effects. Dark corners or alcoves can be illuminated with relatively high-intensity localized light. This provides a natural contrast with main room lighting, helping to counter shadows and also contrasting the 'flatness' which is created by a predominantly overhead lighting system.

**Below:** This decorative brass table lamp with an unusual glass shade really complements the highly ornate side table

even though they illuminate effectively the table upon which the lamp is placed. For TV viewing this arrangement is ideal. There is little reflected light from the screen to cause distraction, yet the room is not in complete darkness, and is less likely to cause any possible eye strain.

Another way of altering the intensity of a lamp is to move its shade around, experimenting to see which way the shadows fall to achieve the best effect.

The only practical restriction on where you can position either table or standard lamps is the location of a suitable power point. Simply using long flex is no answer, especially if it stretches over a walkway.

A sensible approach is to first plan thoroughly where you intend to position lamps and then to introduce power

**Below:** This old-fashioned type of oil lamp has been cleverly converted to use electric power to provide a pretty and decorative light source

**Above:** A free-standing lamp with an adjustable neck and high-intensity spotlight is perfect for a modern setting.
**Left:** This pretty lamp adds a colourful touch to the simple wall display

Equally, table lamps can be used to concentrate light on ornaments, plants and so on, without recourse to the colder light often produced by wall-mounted spotlights or fittings with internally silvered lamp bulbs. Free-standing standard lamps are designed to throw light either upwards or downwards, depending on the shade. Some shades are semi-translucent, which allows some light to go through sideways and gives a softer effect.

With traditional table or standard lamps you can restrict the spread of light by choosing the right type of lampshade. Dense, drum shades will spill light up and down while only a little escapes through the shade's fabric. And dense shades also prevent glare at eye level,

points as close as possible to these locations. It is a good idea for you to add these fittings before, say, you decorate a room.

In some cases in the UK, table and standard lamps can be incorporated into the lighting circuit using approved plugs, sockets and fittings. This leaves the 13 amp ring main circuit free for components which operate at higher wattages.

There is a huge choice of lamps and shades available today. With table or standard spotlights, the units are integral and must therefore complement your interior decoration as a complete assembly. But with more traditional

**Below**: A decorative fringed shade on a standard lamp gives ideal light for reading by and adds character to the room

lamps the style can be altered quite substantially by the choice of shades, both in terms of colour and fabric. Shades can be covered to match the wallpaper or curtain fabric so that they become part of a well-planned and co-ordinated scheme.

Oil, Victorian and art deco lamps are now very popular and there are good reproductions available to give you a considerable choice of colour and different styles. Search around junk shops and antique shops to see if you can find lamps of this type which are suitable.

Remember that free-standing lamps can be relatively inexpensive devices for changing the entire appearance of a room. Whether you need them for practical pupposes or simply to achieve a mood, they can be invaluable for highlighting or disguising special features.

# Lighting outdoors

Well-designed exterior lighting can turn your patio or garden into a night-time wonderland. On warm summer evenings, garden lights enable you to extend your living space outside. And even in colder climates, when there is frost or snow in the air, exterior lighting adds a sparkling new dimension to the view from your windows.

But exterior lights serve more than just a decorative purpose. You can use them to light up a porch and front door; or to illuminate drives and pathways so that visitors can see the way in.

## Choosing exterior lights

The variety of exterior lights and lamps almost equals that of interior lighting. Long gone are the days when you could buy only rather crude floodlights which made the garden resemble a football pitch. Modern exterior lights range in function from spotlamps to hanging lanterns, and in style from old-fashioned brass to ultra-modern bulbous glass.

Wall-mounted lamps which cast a soft, diffused light are suitable for lighting a porch, a patio or even a gate in a garden wall. Many shops sell beautiful old brass lanterns converted for this purpose, and replicas are just as easily available. Cast-iron, cottage-style lamps have a similar function and, with frosted glass windows, lend a Dickensian glow to the porch. More suited to modern-style houses are the cylindrical, circular and oval designs with frosted or clouded glass.

Floodlights and spotlamps, casting a swathe of light through the darkness, can pick out anything from trees to the whole front or rear elevation of the house. You can buy them hooded to restrict the light path, or fully exposed to cast a broader beam.

Mounted in the ground they can be

**Below:** Add drama and mystery to your garden by using spotlights to highlight statues or attractive ornamental features such as dark garden pools or perhaps rockeries

pointed in any direction, in trees they appear as a secret source of light and on a sweeping driveway they can illuminate the house as though it were day.

For lighting paths and driveways—and for any part of the garden, patio or terrace which would benefit from general illumination—there are many kinds of pole-mounted downlighters which cast a diffused light over a fairly wide area. The styles vary from miniature street lights to elegant bowl-shaped lamps perched on tall poles.

## Wiring up

Any exterior light fitting, unless it is sheltered in a porch, must be fully sealed and insulated because it will always be

**Below:** Spotlights are invaluable for garden lighting. They help create a romantic, gentle atmosphere

exposed to the elements—even if it is not always switched on. Porch lights and lamps mounted on exterior walls can generally be connected directly into the interior lighting circuit. But with lights fitted some distance from the house, this is not always possible.

Installing an exterior lighting circuit is a job that requires great care—the results must remain safe even after years of exposure to the weather. If you have any doubts about your skills, let a professional do the job.

Use only fittings—lights, sockets, bulbs and so on—that are designed for outdoor use. Unless your lighting circuit is very simple, wire it to a separate fuse on the fuseboard—the circuit should have its own isolating switch as well. In the UK, you could wire a lighting circuit via a fused switched connection unit, fitted to a spur on the ring main. Use suitable

cable—in the UK, mineral insulated or armoured PVC sheathed, buried at least 450mm below ground, or ordinary PVC cable protected by heavy-gauge conduit and buried at the same depth.

It is sensible to have the circuit checked by a professional before connecting it (or having it connected for you) to the mains.

## Positioning lights

Choosing what to illuminate and where to place the lights is almost as critical as selecting the lights themselves. At all times bear in mind that once you have positioned a light outside and buried the cable, it can be a lengthy job repositioning it. Always experiment with different locations before you make any final decisions—the extra effort will be well worthwhile.

If you simply want to illuminate a drive or pathway, the kind of lights you choose and where you position them will depend mostly on the surroundings. If you have trees lining a sweeping drive or even a narrow path, the lights should be positioned to offer a clear line to the house.

A long drive is often adequately served by just one pole-mounted downlighter near the entrance and another closer to the house. Casting a glow over a wide area, these lamps will create a welcoming atmosphere without being excessively obtrusive.

Remember that a powerful single lamp close to the house can also serve to illuminate the house itself, so here you might consider a spot or floodlamp more effective. Positioned behind a shrub or rockery and pointing upwards to the house, the secret source of light can have a most entrancing and mysterious effect.

Many families now enjoy barbecue parties on warm evenings and some kind of lighting is essential to make the most of the occasion. In a well-appointed patio, there may be separate eating and cooking areas which would best be served by individual lighting of different types.

**Above:** Why not give your visitors a double welcome and clearly spotlight your house number on an outside wall as well as on the front door

Powerful spotlamps pointing up towards the house would undoubtedly create too much glare: softer, glowing lamps which cast a more diffused, softer illumination over a wider area would be a better choice. Position one close to the barbecue as this is where you will need the most light.

If there are surrounding walls, they might be the ideal places on which to mount the lights.

It can be very disconcerting to be confronted by a black gloom just a few feet beyond the patio, so consider adding one or more lights some distance away in the garden. A single lantern in a tree will probably not be enough, particularly in a large area, so experiment carefully with other lights until you achieve a satisfactory compromise for both patio and garden.

Drawing the eye to one or more points of interest in the garden not only relieves the gloom lying beyond the house, it also enables you to make fuller use of the garden when you are entertaining. Just as lighting a driveway introduces a welcoming atmosphere at the front, so lights in the back garden make it a friendlier place.

The shape and texture of many natural

**Above:** Bring your patio to life at night with a brilliant display of outdoor lighting, using spotlights to pick out features, or diffusers for a gentle background glow. However, it is essential to use only special waterproof lights

features in the garden take on quite a different aspect when illuminated at night. A lamp mounted in the trees creates moving patterns of shadows in the slightest breeze, while spotlamps pick out the delicate tracery of the leaves. Patches of rocks and bricks, shrubs and flowers are all enhanced by illumination: try lighting them from spotlamps hidden away in a tree or bush.

Even from inside the house, especially during the colder months of winter when the trees sparkle with frost or are covered by fingers of snow, the garden itself can become a picture in a window frame.

Illuminated from below by spotlamps, a pergola can be transformed into a night-time roof of greenery; because of the effects of shadows, any foliage thickens and becomes glossy—the very shape and proportion of the garden is often altered beyond recognition at night.

But of all the features in a garden that are transformed by exterior lighting, the

most spectacular are pools of water. A fountain or even a pond will sparkle when lit from above by spotlamps. Plants and ornaments in water become more distinctive, goldfish shimmer and the contrast with surrounding shadows is striking.

## Lighting the house
The house itself can benefit from some illumination and again spotlamps work best at picking out the most attractive and decorative features.

Lamps mounted on the walls are not generally very effective in this respect because they tend to cast shadows that distort the exterior features.

It is better to position a pair of spotlamps centrally, some distance from the front of the house, so that they can be angled to either side. This ensures that the entire front elevation is evenly illuminated.

Alternatively, individual spotlamps can be placed at the sides pointing inwards. In both cases, the lights should be positioned at ground level pointing upwards. Take care not to buy excessively powerful lamps (unless you have a very large house) since even the low-powered variety create some glare.

# INDEX

The numbers in **bold** indicate detailed projects and the *italic* numbers refer to pictures.

**Picture credits**
Simon Butcher: 37, 38
Ray Duns: 15, 16, 17, 18, 19, 30, 34, 35, 54/5, 58, 59, 61, 62, 65, 66, 68, 69
Clive Helm: 80
Bill McLaughlin: 73, 76
Rotoflex Home Lighting: 77, 78
Elizabeth Whiting: 1, 74, 75, 79

**Artwork credits**
Advertising Arts: 70, 71, 72
Bernard Fallon: 10, 11, 33, 39, 40, 41, 56, 57
Nigel Osborne: 43, 44, 45, 46, 47
Colin Salmon: 2, 3, 4/5, 6, 7
Venner Artists: 8, 21, 22/3, 26, 30/1, 63